Church and colonialism

Church and Colonialism

Helder Camara

translated by William McSweeney

Sheed and Ward · London and Sydney

First published 1969
Sheed and Ward Ltd, 33 Maiden Lane, London WC2, and
Sheed and Ward Pty Ltd, 204 Clarence Street, Sydney NSW 2000
© Sheed and Ward Ltd 1969

Originally published as *Terzo Mondo Defraudato* by Editrice
Missionaria Italiana, Turin 1968. Chapter 10 was previously published (in French) in *Informations Catholiques Internationales.*

Standard book number: 7220 0567 9 (cloth)
Standard book number: 7220 0564 4 (paper)
This book is set in 11/13 pt Linotype Times
Made and printed in Great Britain by
William Clowes and Sons Ltd, London and Beccles

Contents

Preface

If you'll pardon this personal note, I should like to confess that I've always dreamed of visiting England. Now that some of my speeches are being published in English I shall be able to travel through your country, at least indirectly. It only remains for me to meet the English in person and to talk about England's role in the world today, and in particular about its responsibilities towards the underdeveloped world.

These speeches which are now translated into English are my visiting-card, a brotherly greeting to you. One of these days I may have the pleasure of talking to Englishmen face to face. The English seem to me a great people, especially in the hours of 'blood, sweat, toil and tears'.

HELDER CAMARA

Recife
December 1968

Introduction

On introducing himself, in 1964, to the people of his diocese of Olinda and Recife in north-east Brazil, the new archbishop Dom Helder Camara proposed, among other things, to live collegiality at all levels, to be one with his bishop auxiliary and with the suffragan and other bishops of Brazil and of Latin America, 'one with the bishops of the whole world and with the Holy Father, the guarantee and assurance of collegiality'.

How could the archbishop of Turin, remembering the bond of collegiality, the profound reality of faith and love in common responsibility for the whole church, refuse the friendly invitation of the archbishop of Olinda and Recife to introduce his book?

On reflection, it seems to me that one theme predominates in the pages of this book, recurring with varying stress according to the context and the people who were being addressed: it is a call to humanity, and especially to catholics, to take note of the tragic situation of the underdeveloped world.

No-one is surprised that Brazil, and in particular the North-East, where there is a process of 'development without justice', should be a source of anxiety for a Brazilian bishop. But in the claims and observations which we read in these pages, in the principles which they call to mind and the proposals which they suggest, we are initiated into the vast geography of hunger, two-thirds of humanity condemned to a life of degrading misery. To imagine that this immense panorama can be of little interest to the peoples of wealthier nations would be to repudiate the gospel and the law of solidarity inscribed on the conscience of man.

In the past, the means of communication may have explained our lack of concern for the poor in far-off lands, though it can scarcely justify our indifference. But today we see this tragic reality with a brutal clarity which forces us to take note and seriously to examine our consciences.

This book, in my opinion, will occupy a significant place in the already abundant literature on under-development. Here is the voice of a man, a christian, a bishop, who experiences the situation of his people and measures and judges it by the light of the gospel. Firmly and decisively he condemns selfish profiteering, vainly disguised by a hypocritical concern for order and social security. Elsewhere, applying sound social and economic principles, he does not hesitate to propose concrete remedies for a situation intolerable by human and christian standards.

Dom Helder treats here of the Third World, the underdeveloped world. But it is not difficult to recognise in certain situations which are condemned in these pages the privations and injustices which still prevail in affluent welfare societies.

It is not only to Brazil that we must extend the invitation to management to recognise 'justly and honestly that the worker is isolated without his brother-workers and has little chance of being heard and satisfied'; nor the caution to trade unions not to disqualify themselves by surpassing the limits of justice.

It is not only in Brazil that we find business concerns where everything seems perfect 'regarding job security, wages, education conditions, health and recreation' but where, at every turn, there is an invisible notice: 'Worker, you will be given everything provided you never dream of those middle-class luxuries, intelligence and freedom'.

It is sad to think how far we are from that 'respect for man' which should make 'each of us consider our neighbour, without exception, as another "self"' according to the gospel teaching reiterated by the Vatican Council (*Gaudium et Spes* 27).

May the frank and fervent word of this bishop, who worthily continues the tradition of Basil, Ambrose, Chrysostom, find an attentive ear in the world of today, and arouse an uneasiness which may lead to a new search for the way of justice, love and peace.

Turin, 1st Sunday of Advent 1967

✠ Michele Cardinal Pellegrino, Archbishop

1
Dom Helder Camara introduces himself to his flock

In April 1964 Paul VI designated as archbishop of Olinda and Recife (Olinda is an ancient town lying close to Recife, the capital of north-east Brazil) Dom Helder Camara, then bishop auxiliary to the cardinal of Rio de Janeiro and secretary of the Brazilian Episcopal Conference. Dom Helder addressed the following message to the people of his diocese on taking possession of Olinda and Recife.

No room for compromise

Providence has taken me by the hand and led me to Olinda and Recife; Pope Paul VI, who has a deep knowledge of Latin America and Brazil, decided that this key-position of north-east Brazil should be filled without delay, after the unexpected death of our beloved Dom Carlos Coelho.

It is a divine grace to be able to detect the signs of the times, to be abreast of modern developments, to participate fully in the plan of God. Let us examine together what is taking place. Let us discuss the impressions which strike me at the beginning of my apostolate. Let us touch briefly on initial proposals and first ideas.

On arrival here in 1961, Dom Sebastiano Leme—he too from Rio—published a famous pastoral letter. What would the great Dom Sebastiano say of the Brazilian North-East in 1964? What does our late Dom Carlos suggest? What am I inspired to do by the Holy Spirit who drew me here?

Who am I and who am I speaking to or trying to speak to? I am a native of the North-East addressing other natives of the North-East, with eyes turned to Brazil, to Latin America and to the world. A human creature who regards himself as brother in weakness and in sin to all men, of all races and all religions of the world. I am a christian who addresses himself to christians, but with heart open, ecumenically, to men of every creed and ideology. A bishop of the catholic church who comes, in the imitation of Christ, not to be served but to serve. Catholics and non-catholics, believers and non-believers, all of you accept my brotherly greetings: 'May Jesus Christ be praised!'

The bishop belongs to all Let no-one be scandalised if I frequent those who are considered unworthy and sinful. Who is not a sinner? Who can throw the first stone? Our Lord, charged with visiting publicans and eating with sinners, replied that it is the sick who have need of the doctor.

Let no-one be alarmed if I am seen with compromising and dangerous people, of the left or the right, of establishment or opposition, with reformist or anti-reformist, revolutionary or anti-revolutionary, with those of good faith or bad.

Let no-one claim to bind me to a group, so that I should consider his friends to be mine and make my own his hostilities. My door and my heart will be open to everyone, absolutely everyone. Christ died for all men; I must exclude no-one from fraternal dialogue.

Concern for the poor   It is clear that, loving everyone, I must have special love, like Christ, for the poor. At the last judgment, we shall all be judged by our treatment of Christ, of Christ who hungers and thirsts, who is dirty, injured and oppressed.

Continuing the existing work of our archdiocese, I shall care for the poor, being particularly concerned that poverty should not degenerate into misery. Poverty can and at times must be accepted generously or offered spontaneously as a gift to the Father. But misery is degrading and repellent; it destroys the image of God which is in each of us; it violates the right and duty of human beings to strive for personal fulfilment.

It is obvious that I am thinking in a special way of the *mocambos*[1] and the abandoned children. Whoever is suffering in body or in spirit, whether he is rich or poor, whoever is desperate, shall have a special place in the heart of the bishop.

But I do not wish to deceive anyone, as though a little generosity and social assistance were sufficient. Without a doubt there are spectacular miseries which give us no right to remain indifferent. Often the only thing to do is to give immediate help. However, let us not think that the problem is limited to certain slight reforms and let us not confuse the good and indis-

[1] This is the name given to the slum areas of Recife.

pensible notion of order, the goal of all human progress, with caricatures of it which are responsible for the persistence of structures which everyone recognises cannot be preserved.

Pioneering the way to development If we wish to tackle the roots of our social evils, we must help our country to break the vicious circle of underdevelopment and misery. Some people are scandalised that this should be our primary problem. Others question the sincerity of our motives.

One day, at a meeting of government technicians, the bishops of the North-East appealed to them to combine our small resources and our few specialists who were engaged in isolated undertakings. This pioneer attitude gave rise to the Centre for the Development of north-east Brazil (SUDENE, as it is called) which, we hope, will be instrumental in correcting the criminal imbalance between highly-developed and depressed areas. It deserves our support. By means of SUDENE the use of foreign capital in a manner befitting national dignity has been made possible and, what is more encouraging, a reversal of the situation in the North-East has been initiated. But let us not deceive ourselves. Development cannot come from above, it cannot be imposed. It demands awakening the conscience, arousing public opinion, stimulating education, self-improvement, technical planning.

The church is not marginal to history. She lives at the heart of things through a free, mature and responsible laity. Christ gave to the hierarchy a mission which is specifically evangelical, but this does not mean that the christian community must separate itself from the great adventure of progress. On the contrary, christian laymen must be responsible for manning the front line. We have great trust in those christians who witness to Christ by their involvement in social problems. Today it is essential to apply ourselves to technical planning in all its complexity. It is equally essential, therefore, if we are to avoid a bureaucratic technocracy, that the whole community of the North-East should be alive to the situation and take an active part in the planned development of their region. The formation of management teams in all sectors is imperative. And because of the human wealth of the people of the North-East we can be sure that they will find their development in the soil and the climate which God has given them. Let us all cooperate in making the North-East a community in development, open to Brazil and to the world.

A moment's reflection   Let us pause and reflect for a moment, for the sake of those who are alarmed at our thoughts or irritated by our language and ideas.

God has directed the intellect towards truth. We can only assent to error because we are attracted by the element of truth it contains. The best way to combat error and to destroy its seductive power and inner consistency, is to liberate this element of truth.

We should have the courage and serenity of spirit to preserve sound ideas which are embodied in language which, at the moment, we find unacceptable. Pop-culture, self-awakening, self-improvement: at times we should do well to avoid or change these expressions. But we should never abandon sound ideas because they are sustained by erroneous methods. Why should we fear movements which are concerned with authentic democracy and which can be realised only under a regime which respects liberty? Why should we fear movements which of their nature are profoundly christian?

It would be scandalous and unforgivable if the church were to abandon the masses in their hour of greatest need; they would think we had no interest in helping them to achieve a degree of human and christian dignity and to raise themselves to the category of people.

Human values to be developed   We are all convinced that all men are sons of the same heavenly Father. Those who have the same father are brothers; let us treat one another as brothers.

We are all convinced that God made man to his own image and likeness and entrusted to him the mission of dominating nature and completing the work of creation. Let us do everything possible or impossible that work in the North-East may be truly a participation in the work of our creator.

We are all convinced that freedom is a divine gift which must be preserved at any price. Let us liberate, in the fullest sense of the word, every human creature in our midst.

We are all convinced that our ideal is the development of each and every creature among us. There are not lacking today examples of religious indifference and atheism among highly-developed nations. Our own development project does not seek to exclude God. The more we progress materially, the greater will be our need of a strong, clear faith capable of illuminating from within the construction of the new North-East.

For the present all this is rather vague. But we shall be living together, with the grace of God. We shall examine in depth each of these affirmations. We shall study ways of realising them. But for all this, let us repeat again and again that the church will not be allied to any person, party or movement of a political or economic character.

The church has no wish to dominate the course of events. She is here to serve men, to help them be free. And she will be ready to affirm that this process of liberation, which begins in time, cannot be fully accomplished until the end of time, the true beginning when the Son of God returns.

You will have noticed that the North-East is at once a national problem and a centre of international attention. But the image which is presented of us, both at home and abroad, is invariably false.

The christian responsibility of the North-East

The world looks to the North-East   By now the North-East is a cliché, a slogan. The North-East does not accept this standardisation of misery, and cannot, must not, accept classification as the most explosive area of Latin America.

Let us be united in making the North-East an anticipation of tomorrow's Brazil, of the future Latin America and of the new face of the Third World. Let us be united because no authentic development can be restricted to one group or to one class. Either the entire region is developed, with all its human groupings, or development is distorted.

10

It is for this reason that I make no appeal to management and workers, to rich and poor, to left and right, to believer and non-believer, that they should agree on a truce. It is essential to begin, trustingly, a crescendo of dialogue. It would be a grave matter before the judgment of God and of history to withdraw oneself from the reconstruction of the world.

The christian portion of the Third World   Integrated still more with Brazil and Latin America, we bear the responsibility of being the christian portion, the christian continent, of the Third World. Clearly we do not claim to be superior or better than our Asian and African brothers. But we have greater responsibility.

Our christianity must inspire us to serve in such manner that our progress and development shall not make us egoistic or overbearing. This remark is not without reason. We must never forget that the slogans against foreign imperialism which cover our walls are directed against Brazilian imperialism in cities like the capitals of Bolivia and Paraguay. On the part of christian Latin America, the witness to Christ most clearly understood by our African and Asian brothers will be a true brotherhood within the continent, a fraternal exchange with the Third World and fraternal dialogue with the world already developed.

Christ is José, António, Severino   Let us press on without delay with the task of development as a christian means of evangelising. What value can there be in venerating pretty images of Christ, or even recognising his disfigured face in that of the poor, if we fail to identify him with the human being who needs to be rescued from his underdeveloped condition.

However strange it may seem to some, Christ in the North-East is called José, António, Severino ... Behold the man! This is Christ, the man who needs justice, who has a right to justice, who deserves justice. If we are to avoid sterile and destructive violence on the part of the oppressed, we must look beyond the appearance of harmony which makes dialogue impossible.

Instead of feeling resentment that the worker should look to the trade unions for support, management should recognise, justly and honestly, that the worker is isolated without his brother-workers, and has little chance of being heard and satisfied. And the trade unions, on their side, disqualify themselves morally when they surpass the limits of justice. The abuse of power on the part of management must not lead to an abuse of power on the part of workers. Dialogue demands mutual respect and a minimum of trust and goodwill.

Brazil today offers immense scope and countless opportunities to anyone with a generous heart. Having within her boundaries developed and developing areas (or shamelessly and scandalously underdeveloped, even abandoned areas) she can and must proclaim to the world the most important dialogue of our time: that between developed and underdeveloped.

Everyone knows and shouts about the need for radical reform in our country. In the past there has been mistrust of the reformers and the constant fear of communist infiltration. Now that the situation has changed there is no time to lose. The desired reforms must come without delay. Let them be just and balanced, but on no account must they give the impression of mystification.

The reforms should come in a spontaneous way and, above all, without rancour or ill-feeling. Let the Brazilian people be incapable of hatred, realising that this is the greatest sin, since God is charity, God is love.

As for the North-East, which begins its development against a background of depressions and hopes, let it be an example to the whole country of a dynamic peace founded on justice, of truth rooted in charity, of dialogue and understanding among brothers which transcend divisions capable of dragging the country into civil war and chaos.

Let the North-East be an example to the whole of Brazil of a speedy recovery from political crisis. Without prejudice to national security measures or vigilance towards communism, let us not accuse of communism those who simply hunger and thirst for social justice and the development of our country. Let us help Brazil not to destroy the hopes of the people. We shall prove that democracy is capable of tackling the very roots of our social evils.

General policy

The time of the Council   It is a serious responsibility to live in the time of the second Vatican Council. Pope John XXIII inaugurated it as a council with a difference, one which was not concerned to condemn or anathematise, since doctrinal errors were already more than condemned.

The task of the council was to reform the church, which is divine in origin but entrusted to frail and sinful men. According to Pope John, the church will facilitate the reunion of christian families and will attract countless men of goodwill in the measure in which she renews and reforms herself. Pope Paul VI thinks and acts in the same way.

To the priests, religious and laity of the archdiocese, I propose this directive of the council. Instead of trying to reform others, let us first reform ourselves. The difference between a pharisee and a saint is that the pharisee is big-hearted with himself and strict with others, trying to force them into heaven. The saint is rigorous only with himself; with sinners he is generous as the goodness of God, boundless as the mercy of the Father.

The time of collegiality The decision of the Vatican Council to implement the gospel teaching of the collegiality of bishops under the primacy of the pope is a significant step towards renewal.

We shall try, with God's help, to live this collegiality; to be one with our auxiliary Dom José Lamartine, one with the suffragan bishops of the province of Olinda and Recife, with the episcopal secretariat of the North-East, with the National Conference of Brazilian Bishops and with the Latin-American Episcopal Council; one with the bishops of the whole world and with the Holy Father, the guarantee and assurance of collegiality.

In our diocese, episcopal collegiality will be completed by the body of priests, by the community of the bishop and his diocesan clergy, in sincere and holy union with the religious. I want my priests to know that we shall achieve, by the grace of God, a complete brotherhood and an atmosphere of solidarity, trust, maturity of dialogue and of service. It is easy to imagine what the seminary means to one who speaks like this of his priests; priests and seminarists will have the best part of our time.

As regards the sisters, I can see that from now on they will be quite indispensable to our plans for the apostolate. With absolute respect for the spirit of each order and congregation, it is evident that areas undergoing complete transformation like the North-East are ripe for the apostolic renewal as envisaged by the great Cardinal Suenens.

We have spoken elsewhere, in the strongest terms, of the role of the layman. There is no substitute for his mission in the church, which is to witness to Christ in every work of civilisation. Here let it be added that we shall respect his freedom of choice; diverse positions and diverse opinions in the questions under discussion demonstrate a spirit of initiative and a search for authenticity. This is not a breach of unity but rather a desire to live in different ways the meaning of the incarnation. It can only be hoped that mutual respect and charity will prevail wherever differing points of view can reasonably be adopted, and that in the higher truths all will find agreement. May our beloved Catholic Action Movement, from which so much more is expected, be constant in striving for unity.

All of us—clergy, religious and laity—let us form in Christ the community of the church which is open, welcoming, eager for sincere dialogue.

The time of ecumenism Being moved still by the spirit of the council, we encourage all our people to keep in mind at all times—in our reunions, in our studies, in our prayer—not only those of other religions, but also those who are unaffiliated to any church. I have a particular regard for people of no faith, who wander in darkness, especially when they are atheist in name but christian in deed.

To those who constitute 'the world', as we call it, I repeat the inspired words of Paul VI in the inaugural address at the second session of the Vatican Council: 'Let the world know that the church looks on it with profound understanding, with sincere admiration and with the genuine intention not of conquering it, but of serving it; not of despising it, but of appreciating it; not of condemning it but of strengthening and saving it.'

The devout who hear my words are probably thinking that their bishop is more concerned with the strayed sheep than with the ninety-nine who never abandoned the flock. But isn't this precisely the attitude of the Good Shepherd?

Obviously we shall have time also for our revered and devoted faithful. Our work with them will be inspired by the transfiguration of the Lord, the title of our archdiocese: by our baptism we are made one with Christ; instead of a worn and faded Christ, it is necessary that he be transfigured in us as he was on Mount Tabor. Our Lady, patroness of Olinda and Recife, will assist in the glorification of her Son in and through us.

Do you remember the moving spectacle at the death of Pope John XXIII? This unforgettable scene is, I am sure, a lesson for all of us. Catholics and non-catholics, believers and non-believers, men of all races, creeds and ideologies suffered with the pope in his last agony and lamented his death as the death of a father, thereby manifesting the implicit desire of the people: a prelate, a bishop must be good like Pope John.

Pray to your heavenly Father, the giver of every grace and every light, that this may be the livery of your new bishop; that he may remind you of Pope John XXIII. This will be an excellent way of reminding you of Christ himself, the Good Shepherd.

2
Towards a christian vision of development

The following address was given on 2 May 1965, in the presence of Mgr Antonio Samoré, vice-president of the Pontifical Commission for Latin America, and of many other prelates, on the occasion of the inauguration of the regional seminary of north-east Brazil, constructed near Recife.

The realism of the church   The Holy See desired, and then constructed, this regional seminary of the North-East which your Excellency, on behalf of Pope Paul VI, offered to the heavenly Father in the eucharistic sacrifice, and which you will solemnly inaugurate within a few moments. We shall express our gratitude to the pope by speaking of the great sign to be seen in this institution and the programme of life and work which the regional seminary suggests to us.

Obviously, here as elsewhere, the seminary is an institution for the formation of priests; and here, as in every part of the globe, the essential mission of the priest is to proclaim the message of salvation. But the church, the continuing presence of Christ, has a sense of reality; she knows what she is up against; she knows what she must do—here, now, in the circumstances of time and place in which she finds herself. The regional seminary is being inaugurated in 1965, in Recife. Anyone with eyes to see will realise that the seminary is being opened in the heart of the Brazilian North-East when the ten-year development scheme is already begun.

Development is a high and noble idea, even if hitherto mutilated in its essence and sacrificed in its implications. It is already something when economic development is complemented by social development. It is already something when the development of a region gives way to the global expansion of a country.

The regional seminary is born with the responsibility of enriching the concept of development with all its vast human significance, and of adding to it the new dimension which the supernatural brings to human limitation. In such a problematic situation, one can appreciate the clear-sightedness of Rome in erecting this seminary, a discreet and sure way of being present to the situation of development—the most universal and urgent problem which humanity today must face.

Evangelisation and humanisation This building will prepare priests for preaching the gospel. But the gospel is not preached to abstract beings without the limitations of time and space. One evangelises actual human creatures living at a point in space and time.

So when our seminarists arrive at the churches and chapels and speak about divine grace—which is the presence in us of the Trinity and which makes us sharers in the divine life—how can they forget that divine life is being proclaimed to people in sub-human conditions? When they speak of the heavenly Father— our heavenly Father who makes us all brothers—they will proclaim an illusion which life will show up in an appalling manner.

It is too easy to multiply examples of this kind. To persist in pure spiritual evangelising would be to give, within a short time, the idea that religion is a theory separated from life and incapable of touching it or modifying its absurdities. Among other things, it would support the view that religion, the great estranged and the great alienator, is the opium of the people.

Evangelisation in the name of Christ, in a region like ours, aims at humanisation in the fullest sense. The boundary between the two fields is purely theoretical— with respect of course for the distinction from a theological point of view.

And we bishops of the North-East—with our clergy, religious and laity—let us strive wholeheartedly for development. It would be pharisaical to be uninterested in economic expansion. One day we asked the government technicians if they would agree on a global plan for the region, an indispensable starting point for breaking the barrier of underdevelopment. Immediately we felt called to help in preparing the people for development, making sure that it should not come from above, drop ready-made from the heavens to fatten our wealthy technocracy.

And we began the Movement for Basic Education, using the transistor radio to reach remote villages not as yet electrified, in order to give the masses the foundation for their human and christian fulfilment. More important than the rudiments of formal education is the task of putting people on their feet, of opening their eyes, of making them aware. If we omit this—the expression recalls the sin of omission—then tomorrow their eyes will be opened without us and against us. They would consider that they had been abandoned by the church which was a coward in the face of the powerful, an accomplice of the wealthy who concealed tremendous injustice with generous cult offerings and donations to christian social activities.

And we bishops of the North-East find it necessary to stimulate rural trade unionism, the only means by which the peasant can state his case to the gentry, who often, if not always, betray in this twentieth century a mentality which is medieval.

Have we departed from our mission? Have we forgotten the proclamation of authentic salvation which we are celebrating in this paschal season? Not at all. We recognise that, as regards temporal problems, we bishops are faced with the theological reflection which will illuminate the work of the laity, whose mission here is quite specific and irreplaceable.

We have no thought of finishing with economic development. We began with that because the Father did not make us pure spirits. We are obliged not to leave to the laity a work which would normally be of christian presence in the world, because we feel that in the face of short-sightedness, indifference and arrogance, it is necessary to lend support to the elementary work of defending human rights. And if people have the audacity to refer to the bishops of the church as 'communists', the bishops who are dedicated to the christian mission of defending broken human persons, what will they do to our priests and above all to our laity, if we abandon them to their lot?

However, while we must always begin at the practical level of economic development, our religious convictions and our love for creatures move us to desire for them much more than what is simply economic or even social. Our motto for development is the saying of Christ: 'I am come so that they may have life and have it to the full.' We shall not rest until the North-East passes from underdevelopment to fullness of life in the grace of God, which completes and transcends the limits of the human and makes us sharers in the divine nature.

It is exciting to work in the North-East. To say that we are still in a phase of underdevelopment in 1965, does not mean that we forget the situation in 1964, when Brazil reinvested 3% of her gross national product and investment in the North-East, increased to 6% by dint of regional projects; which shows the region's capacity for response. To affirm that we wish to lead the North-East to full development does not imply that we forget the noble religious ideals of which this seminary is a sign.

Global significance of our mission It is time to examine more closely the apparently triumphalist sequence: the mission of Recife in the North-East; of the North-East in Brazil; of Brazil in Latin America; of Latin America in the world.

When we Latin Americans compare our problems with those of Asian and African countries who are liberating themselves from colonialism, we are surprised to discover many points of contact in the difficulties we have to face; we are mature enough to measure the distance between political and economic independence; we are mature enough to understand the diverse and, at times, subtle modalities of neo-colonialism.

If today we compete and clash with other continents on account of the immediate struggle for life, there will come the day when, finally, we shall discover the profound reasons for transforming the realities of the Third World.

If this is true, it is no less true that there exists a spiritual bond between Latin America and the affluent countries because—the reason is frightening—the prosperous part of the world is christian or of christian origin; in other words, 20% of humanity benefits from 80% of world production.

It is sad to think that our African and Asian brothers invariably have an impression of christianity as the religion of the white man: of those who dominated yesterday and even today, who are not committed to anything more than crumb-throwing assistance (never more than 1% of their gross national product); of those who through ambition and vanity, or the illusion of defending human dignity and liberty, compete in an arms race which militates against every programme of aid for development; of those who, through price impositions and taxes on native products, continue to take much more than they offer.

The christians of Latin America have a tremendous responsibility. First towards our christian brothers of the affluent countries: to help them, in charity, to free themselves from egoism; from the excess of comfort and the acceptance of the ephemeral; from practical materialism; from the danger of scandalising our non-christian brethren by giving them a false notion of Christ and of his teaching. Second towards ourselves, to keep our eyes open in the fight for development; to save ourselves from the marxist spell which operates powerfully among the workers and in the universities; to profit from the lesson which the ethics of development desperately calls to the attention of the affluent nations. Ours is the responsibility to experiment with a new dimension of development—the christian dimension. We must lift ourselves out of the sub-human situation of misery without falling into the inhumanity of super-comfort and super-luxury.

Brazil bears in her own flesh the contradiction of the world. Our country has within her boundaries the developed South, and all the rest, North, West-Central, North-East, in course of development. When we can convince the developed South that the most intelligent thing she can do is to bring about full development in the other areas—for then and then alone can she organise her home market, vital for production—Brazilians will have the experience and moral strength to intervene in the dialogue between the developed and the developing world.

Why shouldn't our people be an example of a development, lived and experienced as a transition by the whole population and by each sector of it, from a less human to a more human stage? Why shouldn't our people proclaim the right to development and consequently confront the problem of underdevelopment less in terms of help and favour and more in terms of justice?

Let us not lose ourselves in a mist of words. 'The less

human stage' is an expression implying all the deficiencies which degrade humanity: from material deficiency to moral and spiritual deficiency. It is an expression which tends to any type of oppressive structure—whether we are dealing with abuse of power or abuse of wealth; with corrupt administration; with exploiting the workers; with crooked dealing; with the gambling of speculators.

'The more human stage' is synonymous with a vital minimum of food, health, housing, clothing, education, conditions of work, spiritual care. It is also, and especially, faith in the heavenly Father, in the person of Christ, in the exercise of charity.

Why shouldn't our people give the example of firmly and decisively tackling economic development, completing it with social development and opening out prospects for an expansion which only the grace of God can accomplish?

The role of the regional seminary of the North-East
At this point it can easily be understood and accepted that the regional seminary of the North-East is destined to form priests for development, in the fullest sense of the term. In this house they will study problems connected with the philosophy and theology of development. For example:

How far can you apply to the rich nations the statements of scripture and of the fathers about individuals who are rich?

Is it possible to speak of a 'right to development' in the proper sense of the expression?

What is the precise meaning of the 'right of ownership' in St Thomas Aquinas, the fathers, the magisterium?

How do you mark christian presence in elaborating the global development of a civilisation?

In this building the old theological and philosophical themes will be examined together with the new, against the background of ecumenism and the Vatican Council, and in the light of experience of the Third World. For example:

Revision of the principle of subsidiarity, according to the region to which it applies.

Study of the search for a new socialism.

Clergy and laity in the developed and in the developing world.

Automation and its human implications.

Meanwhile, as the seminary tries to shoulder the responsibility in history entrusted to it by God, the people of God dwelling in this region will become aware of the living forces of the North-East, so that together they may help this portion of the Third World to lift itself from depression.

Utopia? God does not command success. It rarely depends on us. Our job is witness, effort, striving for dialogue.

Years ago, your Excellency, the Holy See, thinking of these and other Latin American problems, set up the Pontifical Commission for Latin America, and since its creation your Excellency has been its life and inspiration.

One day, perhaps, the Holy Father may consider it opportune to enlarge the Commission and transform it into the Pontifical Commission for the Third World, with the clear task of fostering the brotherhood of all humanity.

Two final points Two circumstances must still be mentioned if we are to get a clear picture of the essential reality connected with today's inauguration. Providence has decreed that the seminary should be inaugurated while it is still under construction, and the inauguration is taking place on Good Shepherd Sunday.

Allow me to comment briefly. As regards the inauguration, when as yet less than half the work is completed, consider this symbol: the incomplete seminary, functioning but still under construction. And consider this slogan: the regional seminary will grow with the North-East. Materially and spiritually they will grow in brotherly unity. Thus, in this apparently imposing building, we shall remain faithful to the church, the poor servant.

As regards the Good Shepherd, it is a figure which transcends the ages but is embodied in every era according to the needs of the time. Consider this final image: which sheep does Christ bear on his shoulders as he walks the streets in our days? Just open your eyes and see; the Good Shepherd bears on his shoulders the underdeveloped world.

3
Ten proposals for the Third World

Text of an address given at Amsterdam on the concluding day of the second European Conference of Young Christian Business Executives (December 1965).

Starting almost invariably with concrete facts and proceeding more deeply into the problem of effective collaboration for the development of Latin America and of the entire Third World, I shall state ten propositions, to be followed, in the final brief synthesis, by ten proposals.

A. The problem of development

(1) *Capitalism, the proletariat and proletarian countries*
One day, a European manager of a metalworks in my country asked me to visit his factory, with complete freedom to open all doors and examine all the files and registers. At the end he asked what I thought of his establishment.

I gave him my opinion: 'I think I have seen all that is good in your assembly regarding job security, wages, education conditions, health and recreation. But I cannot understand why there are invisible notices scattered

28

everywhere: "Worker, you will be given everything, provided you never dream of those middle-class luxuries, intelligence and freedom." '

My friend, a good man and intelligent, smiled rather bitterly and commented: 'You are right, but what can I do? Here we are two human beings talking to one another. When I go to a meeting of the Brazilian directors, I am scarcely a fraction of a person, an eighth. When I go to Europe to take part in the general meeting of the company, I am no more than a cog in the machine.'

The problem which confronts business in its relationships with workers is even greater in the proletarian nations of the Third World. It is easy to think of helping the workers provided they do not claim to use their intelligence and their freedom.

(2) *The inhuman investment system* Once in my diocese, a thousand families of fishermen, who were already poor, were in danger of falling into misery. What had happened was that a synthetic rubber plant and a vegetable protein factory had been set up, and the waste chemicals which they threw into the river killed the fish and aggravated the plight of the fishermen. I brought about a meeting between directors and fishermen. The directors explained that within two and a half years their factories would be capable of absorbing the chemical residue. Let them have patience, therefore, for two and a half years. It was useless for the fishermen to complain that within two and a half years they would be made destitute, if they hadn't already died from starvation.

We were facing one of the universal problems of investment, where, in general, the golden rule still prevails: 'Invest where the yield is higher, quicker and surer.' It is too bad if some or many human beings have to be trodden on to apply this rule, but this is the inevitable price of human progress. Or so we are told.

(3) *Not only communism crushes people*   It is clear that communism is not the only force to trample on human beings. In this regard, there is another important consideration. It is moving to observe how developed countries are ready to sacrifice the noblest flower of their youth to save the free world. But when will the developed world become aware of the fact that misery, too, annihilates the human creature, reducing him to sub-human degradation? When will they understand that liberty is a vacuous term for those who live in a dwelling unfit to be called a house; for those who have no food, no clothing, no minimal possibility of education, no real work?

(4) *Help is at most goodwill*   We cannot forget that the developed world comes to the aid of the developing countries. However, without wishing to be ungrateful or to impute less worthy motives to our benefactors, we maintain:

(*a*) that it is bad enough that help hitherto given to the Third World never exceeds 1% of the gross income;

(*b*) that it is bad enough that the arms race is an insuperable obstacle to increasing this contribution;

(*c*) but the worst aspect—and here we have no wish to offend any government, nation or undertaking, but only to invite them to examine their consciences—the worst aspect is that often the money offered is itself stained with the sweat and blood of the underdeveloped world.

(5) *Development synonymous with birth-control?* We should be on our guard against the danger of throwing dust in our own eyes and in the eyes of others every time we are faced with uncomfortable truths. But surely this is the situation of those developed countries who spend a fortune on demographic research and huge campaigns designed to demonstrate that development is synonymous with birth-control? It would be ingenuous to ignore the grave problem of population explosion, whose most tragic effects are felt in the Third World. It would be deceitful to overcome infant mortality only to condemn those saved to a sub-human existence. But anyone who claims to reduce development to birth-control is in need of psychoanalysis.

(6) *Development and food production* No-one can ignore the essential data on world famine. We know, for example, that the world population increased by 11·5% from 1959 to 1964, while food production increased by a bare 6·5%. We know that of the fifty million who die every year, thirty-five million die of starvation or of diseases arising from under-nourishment. Nowadays even children are aware that the map of famine includes Latin America (except Argentina), Africa, the Middle East (except Israel), the Far East (except Japan) and Oceania (except Australia and New Zealand).

That this picture is a slur on our christian civilisation goes without saying. That there is a profound interdependence between hunger and underdevelopment is indisputable. That the apparent super-production of some involves a real under-consumption of others, implying an unbelievable selfishness in those responsible, is a moral problem of the greatest urgency.

But all this cannot authorise anyone to identify nutrition with development as if all that was needed was to distribute to starving countries the agricultural excess of the affluent.

It is better therefore to speak of overcoming hunger by means of development, without forgetting that the hunger of a starving people is not only for bodily nourishment, but also for dignity, responsibility and freedom, and keeping in mind that for the under-developed countries agriculture constitutes the driving force of progress, since they have no other source of revenue.

(7) *Function of foreign technicians and volunteers*
What is to be said of the special type of aid given by the presence in the Third World of foreign technicians and volunteers anxious to collaborate in breaking the most glaring barrier between world and world? I could simply say that the transfer of capital, equipment and battalions of highly-paid technicians has already become part of our experience. But if the people are not prepared for development, and if there are still great masses where there should be an authentic people, then even if development begins, it will immediately dry up and evaporate.

There can be no real development without the humility to be sensitive to local culture, however rudimentary it may be, without attention given to community development, and without that creative and animating participation which is rightly called the corner-stone of development.

But if I left it there and said no more about the presence of technicians and volunteers from overseas, I should have given only part of the picture. There is a more heartening side which leads us to hope for a greater influx from wealthy countries, especially of young people. And this is the deep interest they create, on the part of the developed world, in the problems of the Third World.

When one has a son or a daughter, one's own flesh and blood, in Ghana or Bolivia, in Brazil or in Senegal, then the history of development begins to take on a new dimension. And when the son or daughter returns home, we can be sure that in the former volunteer the Third World will find understanding and sympathy, support and love.

(8) *The need for an awakening*   There is by now the risk of incomprehension, not only on the part of the developed countries but also, and in particular, on the part of certain classes within the developing countries themselves.

Egoism, unfortunately, is not the monopoly of the developed world. In the underdeveloped countries we are still living in the middle ages. With some praiseworthy exceptions, we find among the wealthy the mentality of medieval barons. The days of colonialism are over. But internal colonialism still remains, permitting a quick profit at the cost of keeping the masses in sub-human conditions.

Against such a background, there is a welcome for

the foreigner or the native who shows willingness to help, provided he leaves intact the unjust and sub-human structures, which make the dominating classes the greatest beneficiary of his aid.

Whoever decides to awaken the masses to the absurd, sub-human level of their existence; whoever rises up and demands human and social advancement, which implies a reform of structures, let him prepare himself for slander campaigns, let him expect with certainty to be considered and opposed as a subversive and a communist.

(9) *Is the pressure group justified?*   Love alone constructs. Hatred and violence serve to destroy. What remains, therefore, to the underdeveloped country as a democratic and viable means of opening the eyes of the power classes to the necessity of educating the masses, making them aware of their situation, and disposing them to development and to the indispensable reform of medieval structures? Personally, I favour a large-scale experiment in non-violent action for the whole of the North-East, along the lines of the great movement for racial integration led by Martin Luther King.

When I was very young, I thought Christ was exaggerating when he spoke of the danger of riches. Now I know that it is extraordinarily difficult to combine wealth and human sensitivity. Sooner or later, money covers the eyes with dangerous scales and freezes the lips, the hands and the heart of the creature. From this I draw the conviction that it is democratic and christian to assist human weakness by a balanced, firm and just moral pressure based on non-violent action.

(10) *The reform of commerce* But we shall end by playing with development if we fail to touch the point which could discourage us by reason of its complexity and difficulty: development can only be a plaything if there is no radical reform of the international politics of commerce.

B. The ten proposals

The ten propositions stated above are so much an expression of past and present anxieties that they issue in the following concrete proposals.

(1) All economico-social assistance to proletarian peoples, however vast it may be, demands a freedom from paternalism, and a true and efficacious respect for the intelligence and liberty of the individual and his nation.

(2) In the calculation of investments there must be included a quota related to human needs, so as to avoid the destruction of persons which occurs in the name of progress and development.

(3) As regards communism:

(*a*) We must avoid the pharisaism of a unilateral anticommunism which ignores the equally inhuman character of the capitalist investment policy and forgets that poverty, too, crushes the human person and renders fatuous the divine gift of freedom.

(*b*) We must keep in mind that the best way to combat communism is to tackle courageously and decisively the most urgent problem of our days: the persistence and constant aggravation of the condition of two-thirds of humanity in underdevelopment and starvation.

(c) When we can accept calmly and courageously that socialism and capitalism defy definition in the singular (because socialism has given way to socialisms and capitalism to capitalisms), then we can take the important step for humanity of distinguishing, in certain socialisms, between the economic system and the materialist system. This distinction is impossible when we treat of marxist socialism.

(4) As regards the help given to the Third World by wealthy nations, clearly it should not cease when it has merely expressed goodwill but has not yet done more than scratch the surface of the problem on account of its isolation and relative paucity. Let there be a sincere effort to answer the call of Paul VI at Bombay: 'We entrust to you our special message to the world: may the nations cease the race for arms and apply their resources and their energies to giving brotherly assistance to the developing countries.'

(5) As regards the limitation of births, there could be an implied agreement between the developed and underdeveloped worlds. The countries of the Third World will do everything possible, with respect for the psychology and religious convictions of their people, to achieve responsible procreation. The developed countries, who have a decisive influence on international bodies, will do everything possible to dispel the equivocation which identifies birth-control with development and to remove the absurdity of indiscriminate contraception campaigns which damage respect for the family.

36

(6) The dispatch of food to starving countries should be undertaken not only with discretion, taking advantage of past experience and errors committed in good faith, but also with a just and reasonable measure of assistance given to agriculture, in accordance with the work of the Food and Agriculture Organisation.

(7) Without forgetting the importance of recruiting local workers and technicians of a high standard—technicians capable of giving life to the community—let us have more technicians and volunteers from the wealthy nations, especially the young. Tomorrow, when they return home, the young will constitute the avant-garde of a peaceful but profound social revolution of the developed world, without which we shall never achieve the harmonious and integral development of the entire world.

(8) Let the Young Christian Business Executives of Europe address an urgent and insistent appeal, in continental dialogue, to their brother executives of the underdeveloped countries, that they may understand and accept the self-awakening of the Third World, which is authentic only if constructive, efficient only if it leads to reform of inhuman structures.

(9) Non-violent action, the peaceful weapon of the developing countries, will need the support, at certain times, of the developed world. Take care that the rising masses do not lose confidence in democracy, but that they may trust in love, justice and peace.

(10) If what I have said seems excessive, I shall forget the first nine proposals, so that the tenth, with which I

now close this address, may be carried out to the full, precisely because it touches the core of the subject.

Let the Young Christian Business Executives accept the impossible challenge of undertaking the radical reform of the international politics of commerce. If today's executives lack the understanding and courage for such an enterprise, let them at least prepare the executives of tomorrow for this cyclopean undertaking.

Let them not fear to oppose the great combines, who are more powerful than the mightiest states and whose dealings cry to heaven, especially in the developing countries. Let them know that exploitation by international combines—which kills incipient local industry —sucks from the poor countries more than it gives and threatens to install automation in our underdeveloped areas; that exploitation by international combines is debasing the concept of private initiative and fomenting unjust and indiscriminate hatred against the propertied classes.

Young Christian Business Executives, citizens of the Atlantic, may the blessing of God and your own efforts change the separating waters of the ocean into seas of a civilisation in harmonious and integral development.

4
The Third World and the developing countries

The text of this interview of Fr Piero Gheddo with Dom Helder Camara was prepared for L'Osservatore Romano *during the second session of the Vatican Council (November 1963) together with similar interviews with bishops from the whole world. It was never published. The interview took place at* Domus Mariae, *where Dom Helder resided during the council, and is here reproduced in full.*

'Ours is a time of dialogue. Frontiers and barriers of every kind, which have for so long divided peoples, are now collapsing, and men are meeting one another, speaking to one another, taking steps to know and understand one another. A dialogue is being established between exponents of different philosophies of life, between nations separated by race, language, culture and religion. Above all there is a dialogue between developed and underdeveloped peoples, and the church must be present to illuminate it and guide it towards the goal of charity and justice.'

Dom Helder Camara speaks much about dialogue,

and it is important to know something about the man if we are to understand his ideas. He has an extraordinary gift for understanding others, and could create a bond of sympathy, as I well know, with someone who spoke only Chinese or Tamil. Slight and diminutive in stature, with unusually warm and expressive features, he speaks his own 'peculiar brand of French', as he says himself, accompanying his words with generous explanatory gestures. He speaks with simplicity and immediacy, and the communicative force and relentless logic of his language is such that an interviewer finds it almost impossible and unnecessary to question him.

Auxiliary bishop of Rio de Janeiro, vice-president of the Episcopal Council of Latin America, Dom Helder has a reputation as 'the bishop of the slums', a title which praises his pastoral and social activity on behalf of the deprived inhabitants of the suburbs which skirt the Brazilian capital; the ideal representative therefore of the vast world of underdeveloped peoples, two-thirds of humanity, to be precise. At a press conference held during the council at the Dutch Information Centre, the Brazilian prelate expressed some very interesting ideas on the problem of underdevelopment and on the need for dialogue between rich and starving. One quiet afternoon, when he was not too busy with council affairs, I interviewed him on this very subject.

Interviewer Your Excellency, what can christians do to foster this dialogue?

Camara First of all, they can make Europe and America conscious of the problem of hunger and misery in the world, in all its enormity and drama. You

40

see, I was born in Brazil, in the North-East, an area completely underdeveloped. Our country is as big as a continent and we have the situation of a virtually developed South which covers only a third of the whole country. The remaining two-thirds are 'in course of development', a euphemistic expression which means that the people are still victims of misery and starvation, or at least constant malnutrition. And this seems to be the situation in the whole world: a third of the world population has achieved a level of life worthy of a human being, while the remaining two-thirds still live at sub-human level. This is the reality which christians must bring home to themselves and to others.

I. What does life at sub-human level mean?

C. You need to have seen it to understand fully. It is one thing to read statistics and hear vivid descriptions, quite another to see it with your own eyes. Take the case of a man, the father of a family, who lives in sub-human conditions in an underdeveloped country. This man and his family have no real home, there is insufficient food, their clothing is almost indecent and they have neither the health nor the means to get more; the father has no real work, they are all illiterate and they can see no genuine hope of improvement in the future. This is sub-human living! But there is more to come. You can speak of man with soul and intelligence and freedom. But it seems to me that these divine gifts are luxuries for people like this. What good is intelligence to this man? What does freedom do for him? You often hear it said that we must respect the human person, the liberty of the individual. Absolutely true, but we should add that certain preliminary conditions are essential if the human person is to express himself, if intelligence and liberty are to have any value. For anyone who lives in a state of undernourishment, of chronic diseases, of ignorance and despair, everything atrophies, human dignity, intelligence, the sense of personal freedom.

I. What can be done, your Excellency, to remedy this pitiable situation?

C. What can be done? I shall try to give some points for christians to put into practice according to the possibilities and circumstances of their lives. First it is imperative, in the name of the gospel, to make the underdeveloped masses aware of their human dignity, of their rights, because it is impossible to elevate them to a human level until they are conscious of living at a sub-human level, until they are aware of their right to a better life, one which is worthy of man. This is our christian duty, quite apart from all local and contingent circumstances. It is our duty as christians and bearers of the message of Christ, even if there were no agitation and revolutionary intrigue (and there is), even if communism were not at work (and it is). We must open the eyes of the deprived masses to their misery, and tell them: No, the life you live is not just, something must be done.... Yes, I know well that this attitude is fraught with difficulties and complications. We are told: Why open their eyes if there is no concrete possibility of reform, of achieving a higher standard of living? You are preparing the way for revolt, for communism. And then? My answer to this is that the eyes of the masses are being opened whether we like it or not, with us, without us, against us. It is ingenuous to try to halt a movement which is by now uncontrollable. When a river is in full flow, either you channel it in the right direction or it sweeps away everything. Today's underdeveloped peoples can see for themselves and compare their life to that of the rich in their own country and abroad.

A radical change of attitude

I. This self-awakening is clearly not sufficient to solve the problem. What else can be done?

C. The second point is to stir the conscience of the rich, at home and abroad. I do not know the wealthy in foreign countries and should prefer not to generalise. But I know those in my own country. Let me give you an example. A big landowner invited me to celebrate mass at his establishment. All his workers were there, hundreds of them. If I preach and say, for example, that one must obey one's employer, that one must work with patience and goodwill and do one's duty, for this landowner I am 'a tremendous bishop', 'a holy bishop', I can expect to be invited again to preach. But if, while speaking of the worker's duty and the landowner's rights, I have the audacity, yes the audacity, to mention the worker's rights and the landowner's duty, then it is quite a different matter. 'This is a revolutionary, a progressive, he is pro-communist...' And naturally I shall not be invited there again. This is why I say we must stir the conscience of the rich.

I. What do you mean by 'rich'?

C. Yes, this is another problem, wealth and poverty are relative concepts. Certainly in comparison with the starving and underdeveloped we are all rich and there-fore all responsible. This is particularly true in Europe and North America, where manual and clerical workers are neither rich nor poor yet, when their standard of living is measured against the whole of humanity, they are rich. It is *our* conscience, and that of most of Europe and North America that must be stirred. If I know that there are human creatures like me in some part of the world whose life is not worthy of man, of a son of God, who have neither house nor clothing, neither food nor education, then I must do everything I possibly can to help him, to alleviate his suffering to some extent. And note that this is de-manded not in charity alone but in justice, arising from human solidarity, from the fact that we are all sons of God and brothers in Christ, with the same rights to life and to a human level of existence. This imperative is particularly grave and pressing for the christian. Not that he is a better man than others, but he has greater responsibility, in fact the greatest responsibility because he has met Christ.

I. In concrete terms what can European christians do for the underdeveloped countries?

C. I should not speak of 'European christians', but of all the christians of the world, European, Brazilian, Australian. We need to change a number of attitudes. For example, the attitude which reduces the whole problem of hunger and misery in the world to one of assistance. We christians have what I would call an 'assistance mentality', which considers that all social problems can be solved by charity and assistance to the poor. This attitude must be changed; we must work for social justice. I agree that private and public charity and assistance will always be necessary because there will always be the down-and-outs, the misfits, the abandoned, etc. But the true christian social order—and christians in civil life are bound to work for this—cannot be founded on assistance but must be based on justice.

I. And apart from changing these attitudes?

C. There are others—clearly I cannot remember them all. For example, one often hears it said: in making reforms it is essential to preserve the social order. What social order? I cannot speak for the developed countries, but the so-called 'social order' in the underdeveloped countries is nothing but a cumulus of stratified injustices. We are not political revolutionaries, christians are not die-hard extremists, but if something is unjust it must be removed, even if for a long time it constituted part of the traditional social order. Or again one hears it said: but christians defend private property. Yes, we do defend private property. But we must know what we are talking about. What is private property and when can it truly be called private, that is, in need of defence? And how far can we go in defending private property? To the point of leaving masses of people without the barest necessities? No, this is not justice, in my opinion. You see these are concepts which I express off the cuff and it is difficult here to go into the matter very deeply; nor have they yet been developed theologically, morally, socially. You asked me what European christians could do for the underdeveloped countries. Very well, here is one thing they can do: they can deepen our understanding of social justice, of social order, of the concept of private property.

I. Do you not think that these subjects have already been studied?

C. Yes, they have, but no account has been taken of the new problems created by the emergence of the underdeveloped countries. Take social justice, for example. Up to now it has been considered and studied by catholic moralists and sociologists almost exclusively in relation to the social classes of the same country, not on an international scale. And yet there is an international social justice, Pius XII and John XXIII have spoken about it many times. But how should it be applied by the nations? And what can christians do to bring it about? These are questions which have not so far been answered by scientists, moralists, theologians. Take the problem of socialisation in relation to the development of the human person. Here is a subject much discussed in the developing countries, in which the state must, by force of circumstances, intervene in economic and social life. But to what point can it and must it intervene? How can we reconcile socialisation with the freedom of the human person, with private property? And not just in theory, not just in general principles which everyone knows, but in practice, in the actual situations which occur every day in the underdeveloped countries. The dialogue between rich and poor countries must begin at the level of study and then continue in the publication and application of the results of this study. There is room for everyone in this dialogue, and especially, as far as we catholics are concerned, for the theologians, the scripture scholars, the moralists, the sociologists. I dream of the day when the intellectual catholic élite will place itself at the service of the brethren in backward countries, studying the problems inherent in poverty and misery, in international justice and charity, and perhaps putting aside other projects, other theological topics which have had their day, which serve only for academic dissertations without any practical effect on the life of the people. But there is room for journalists, too. Just imagine the effect of an organised campaign by the press of the developed world to help their brothers in backward countries! When there was a tragedy in Longarone a month ago[1] I was very happy to learn that the Italians spontaneously offered generous relief to the survivors of the disaster, one newspaper collecting over a million pounds by means of its letters. Now tragedies like this happen every day in our country. Not tidal waves which destroy a village, but hunger, misery, malnutrition, which mow down innocent victims. These tragedies are perhaps more serious, of greater dimensions, more persistent and without any human hope of solution. If the catholic press, particularly of the European christian countries, were to interest itself more in these problems. . . . But the problems will not be solved by generous fund-raising alone, but rather by bringing about a sympathy and brotherly love between rich and poor. The rest will follow from that.

[1] Over 2000 people lost their lives on 10 October 1963, when a mountain landslide fell into an artificial lake, causing a tidal wave which swept the village of Longarone. [Tr]

I. Do you think that the church as an institution can do something?

C. She is already doing a great deal. Let us not forget that much of the help which is given to underdeveloped countries, especially in the field of health and education, comes from the missionaries sent by the church. By helping the social and education work of catholic missions, christians are helping the developing peoples, and perhaps this is the best way one can suggest to the individual of contributing to the fight against misery. The council will certainly speak about the fight against underdevelopment and the church will reiterate what the popes have repeated many times, especially John XXIII in *Mater et Magistra.* Today we speak of the 'church of the poor'; I should prefer to speak of the 'church at the service of the poor'. In other words, poverty is an evil to be combated, while the spirit of poverty is a good to be acquired, like the spirit of service. Too often in the past the church has appeared to the people to be an organisation of power and magnificence, almost domineering, even though these are not her fundamental characteristics. Underdevelopment and world misery teach us humility and the spirit of poverty, above all the spirit of service to all mankind.

5
What the council
could not say

Address given at Domus Mariae *in Rome during the fourth session of the second Vatican Council, in November 1965.*

I. The council has said much

The Vatican Council has been significant both by what it has said and by what it has not said. It has made a rich contribution to our understanding of the church, bringing into relief the fruitful idea of the people of God, stressing episcopal collegiality, and opening the door to the laity.

It has cleared the way for the renewal of the liturgy. It has spoken fairly and opportunely on the role of the bishop, on the role of the priest and on the apostolate of the laity.

If it has been less effectual on the means of social communications, on the missions and on christian education, it has nonetheless made a notable and historic contribution in the *Decree on Ecumenism* and in the *Declaration on Non-Christian Religions* and *On Religious Freedom.*

As regards the presence of the church in the world, there is at least a beginning of dialogue with all men of goodwill. And this is a great deal. It is the essential.

It is equally important however to see the significance of what the church has not said. She has refused to condemn, convinced that this is more and more a time of dialogue. She has avoided anything that might give the impression of closing the door, of narrow-mindedness, of an attitude lacking in breadth and nobility.

We can and we ought to thank God for these signs of spring, the theological, liturgical, missionary and ecumenical renewal. A spring which perhaps exceeds the dreams of Pope John, the prophet of Vatican II.

II. What the council leaves to us

However it was not the council's task to say everything. Some things are implied which we must make explicit. There are certain conclusions and practical applications which must be arrived at, not by making appeal to the authority of the council, but by the light of its teaching and by the radiance of its spirit.

(a) When the church of Christ feels morally obliged to re-examine her position on freedom of conscience, when the catholic church takes the historic decision to reverse her previous position in order to defend religious liberty, it is clear that she wishes to demonstrate more and more her respect and love for liberty, that liberty which is related, in the natural order, to intelligence, the most noble gift of God.

We must remember that on the occasion of the second Vatican Council, two thousand years after Christ, at the time when the *Declaration on Religious*

50

Freedom is to be promulgated, two-thirds of humanity are in a sub-human condition which does not allow them to understand the true meaning of liberty.

When the church of Christ feels constrained to give new directives on the economic and social order, she is manifesting, once again, her respect and love for order, which is opposed to disorder, confusion, anarchy, chaos.

We must remember that on the occasion of the second Vatican Council and at the time when, as we hope, the *Pastoral Constitution on the Church in the Modern World* is to be promulgated, with its chapter on economic and social life, two-thirds of humanity live in a so-called 'order' which is so unjust and inhuman that it deserves no other title than 'stratified disorder'.

When the church in council shows anguish at the threat of war which every day strikes new terror; when the pope launches his unforgettable appeal to humanity: 'No more war, no more war', one senses the sincere desire of the church, faithful to Christ, for peace in the world.

We must remember that on the occasion of the second Vatican Council and at the time when, as we hope, the chapter on war and peace, an essential part of the *Pastoral Constitution on the Church in the Modern World* is to be promulgated, two-thirds of humanity are immersed in a pre-war situation—under-development, in other words. And today, according to the famous expression of Cardinal Feltin, development is the new name for peace.

(*b*) Can we speak calmly and objectively of two-thirds of humanity without freedom, in a condition of disordered stratification, in a state of pre-war and pre-revolution? Let us hear some unbiased opinions, beginning with John XXIII in his encyclical *Mater et Magistra*: 'Our soul is filled with profound sorrow at a spectacle of infinite sadness: a multitude of workers, in numerous lands and in entire continents, receive wages which compel them and their families to sub-human conditions of life.'

Listen to Paul VI in his Christmas message 1963: 'Even in our days, entire generations of children perish or vegetate on account of unbelievable privations. Hunger provokes disease and misery; these, in their turn, increase the hunger. It is not prosperity which is lacking to innumerable peoples, but the bare necessities. And if no opportune remedies are found, this deplorable phenomenon will increase rather than diminish.'

According to the statistics of the Food and Agriculture Organisation, 'of the fifty million people who die every year, thirty-five million die of starvation, either directly or as a result of diseases arising from undernourishment'.

Why repeat what we all know? What may be new for some of you is the Prébisch report. Let us leave it to a European, Gilbert Blardone, to comment on the data presented by the secretary of the World Conference of Commerce and Development organised in 1964 by the United Nations in Geneva: 'In the period of 1950–1961, foreign capital invested in Latin America rose to $9,600,000,000, while the amount sent back by Latin America to the lending countries rose to $13,400,000,000. Therefore it is Latin America which has lent to the rich countries. The amount of this loan has risen to $3,800,000,000.'

Blardone continues: 'If we add that the losses suffered on account of falling prices of raw materials and rising prices of manufactured products have risen, in this same period, to $10,100,000,000, it will be seen that the money which left Latin America for the rich countries in the course of these years amounts to $13,900,000,000.'

(c) Does my enthusiastic introduction on the opportuneness and the depth of the council's teaching still hold in the light of these terrible truths which make the council seem remote and alien?

Yes, we shall show that it is valid. The famous *Constitution on the Church in the Modern World* speaks as clearly as is possible for a council. It is for us to arrive at the practical conclusions of the council's premises. Clearly these conclusions will not be the same for all the people of God; there are obligations for clergy and obligations for laity, under the guidance of the hierarchy.

But before arriving at practical conclusions, allow me to stress the special responsibility towards world peace of the church in America, in Latin America and in North America.

III. The responsibility of the church in America

(a) *The church in Latin America* I have underlined the particular responsibility of Latin America in trying to establish equilibrium in the world and in promoting justice on a world scale. This depends on the fact that she is in mid-stream between the developing and the developed world.

If one considers that underdevelopment immerses

Latin America and the entire Third World in a situation unworthy of the human creature, which damages the work of creation; if one considers that an internal revolt against christianity will be inevitable in Latin America if the church holds back now, in the hour of oppression and slavery; if one considers that christian Latin America has a grave responsibility to do all in her power to give human and christian witness to Africa and Asia, her non-christian sisters in underdevelopment, then it is the duty of Latin America to examine what must be done in each country and in the whole continent.

(b) *The church in North America*   The responsibility of the United States and of the church in the United States is no less serious. I have not the slightest wish to tell my brothers in the North American hierarchy what to do. But since goods are divided in a case of extreme necessity, then responsibilities are divided in a situation of extreme gravity. Furthermore, by the mercy of God, I am a human being first and a Latin American second, and I am a bishop of the church before I am archbishop of Olinda and Recife.

When the United States is converted to the economico-social situation of the world; when North America decides to re-examine, in depth, the international politics of commerce—the only way to touch the heart of the problem of economic and integral development—on that day the world will be nearer to peace, the peace which is rendered impossible by stockpiles of nuclear weapons.

It could be said that the church in the United States can do nothing in the face of such difficult and complex problems. But perhaps the concrete suggestions which can be made on this subject will be an agreeable surprise.

IV. Concrete measures to be taken

(a) *Proposals for Latin America*   With brotherly trust I suggest that the hierarchy in each country of Latin America, while attending to directly pastoral work and, with this in mind, to the necessity of saving men in actual situations and not disembodied spirits:

(1) should stimulate integral development;

(2) should openly side with the underdeveloped masses, helping them to become a people;

(3) where they have land at their disposal, especially if it is unproductive and not clearly destined for social purposes, they should try to get rid of it for human and social advancement;

(4) should give their moral support, where the case arises, to non-violent action, capable of shaking the weak landowners, who are still living in the middle ages or engaged in internal colonialism;

(5) should stimulate within their countries a real dialogue between developed and underdeveloped areas.

The ideal is that the laity should lead these movements, inspired by the hierarchy. Sometimes the situation requires that the bishop in person should take part and lend his moral force to safeguard a fundamental right.

Is it too much to ask that the Latin American hierarchy should together inspire, stimulate and follow up a new 'bolivarism'[1] directed, this time, not to political independence but to economico-social independence?

When Latin America faces the attacks of the powerful international combines, and when regional and continental blocs close up in self-defence, a common market will be necessary for Latin America, drawn up, I hope, with the whole Third World, and open, in exemplary fashion, to a just commerce with the entire world.

But perhaps it is only the moral force of the church which can help the Latin American countries to overcome the natural vanity of an adolescent people, and lead them to accept a status of interdependence. Otherwise each and all of the countries will be deprived of the conditions necessary to fight the unequal battle against international greed and selfishness.

(b) *Proposals for North America* The United States can be influenced by public opinion in the following fields:

(1) the universities which study, through their economico-social faculties, the basis for a reformulation of a human and just international politics;

(2) the media of communication (press, radio and television) which, thanks to intelligent and objective reporting, makes the North American public aware that political colonialism is finished, but economic colonialism remains a serious and stifling reality;

[1] Simòn Bolívar (1783–1830) was the great liberator who attempted to free Latin America from colonial domination and unite its people under one government. [Tr]

(3) the groups of workers and businessmen, young and old, who are demanding that the anti-trust laws operating in the United States should apply to trade with the Third World;

(4) the groups of politicians, executive and legislative, who are particularly important since they are in the area of decision-making;

(5) the spiritual leaders of various religions, whose words resound in the consciences of many.

The help in food, men and money given by the North American hierarchy to the entire Third World, and especially to Latin America, is certainly worthy of mention; but even more welcome would be help given to this movement of public opinion, which would assist the United States to take the lead in a revision of life by the whole of Europe.

Pope Paul VI is personally sensitive to the problems of justice and peace, and is constantly alive to the situation in the world. He feels, without doubt, that there is a dramatic lack of authority thoughout the world. When the pope left Rome during the ecumenical council and went to the United Nations, he did so more in terms of service and love than of prestige and power; he knew that he was a pilgrim whose voice had a resonance beyond the frontiers, beyond the barriers, beyond all extremisms, beyond all divisions.

He feels that just as God in moments of acute crisis and of public safety has always raised up shepherds to liberate cities or entire regions from slavery or from death, so today, when injustice is measured on a world scale, and the starving and seething masses are increasing every day and world peace is threatened as never before, the church must be mobilised to assist in the salvation of humanity.

If the hierarchy in every country of the developed and underdeveloped world—and especially in America —without pretensions to prestige or monopoly or leadership, and with the direct support of the pope, stands up with the other spiritual leaders and demands justice as the indispensable condition for peace, and stimulates a real dialogue between the worlds, then we shall arrive in time, perhaps, to help the world and save it from the gravest catastrophe which it has ever suffered.

V. Overcoming the threat of communism

You may feel that this address is misleading and erroneous. Misleading because it keeps quiet about communism which oppresses more and more countries and clearly threatens to extend its influence. Misleading because, while referring to the equivocations of capitalism which praises liberty but then crushes it, praises order and upholds a pseudo-order based on injustice, praises peace yet provokes a pre-war situation —with all this the author says nothing of the deceits of communism which also empty of meaning expressions like 'democracy', 'of the people', 'liberty' and 'peace'.

Perhaps I am completely deceived. But it seems to me that communism will disappear in a remarkable manner when spiritual leaders are moved, not by secret ambition or machiavellianism, but by the crisis of humanity, to take up the defence of the human person. Then, ecumenically united, they can lead the world to harmonious and integral development under the banner of peace based on justice.

At least in our Third World—and perhaps the same is true even of countries under communist rule—communists with a philosophical basis and materialist conviction, communists who are militant atheists, are a minority within a minority.

The great mass of communists will be happy when they realise that it is not necessary to deny God and eternal life in order to love man and fight for justice on earth. The great mass of communists will give to religion their attention and sympathy when they see it resolved never to give cover to absurd injustices committed in the name of the right to property and private initiative.

The great mass of communists will be pleasantly surprised to discover that the gospel inspires a thirst for justice and a desire to end the absurd situation of two-thirds of humanity sinking deeper every day into underdevelopment and starvation.

If some communist leaders are extreme materialists, rooted in hatred and closed up in a militant atheism, there will be another star to guide all men of goodwill without fear of betraying the human cause: the star which proclaimed the birth of the Saviour of mankind.

6
The rise of the new humanism

The full text of a conference held by Dom Helder Camara on 19 June 1967 in the auditorium of the Brazilian newspaper Folha de S Paulo, *which published the original text on 20 June 1967.*

Universal solidarity is one of the dominant ideas of the encyclical *Populorum Progressio*. From the beginning of the encyclical Paul VI proclaims the first decision of the church, especially after the self-awakening of the Vatican Council, to place herself at the service of men, to help them to realise the importance of united action in this decisive moment of human history.

All the second part of the encyclical is given, as we know, to concern for the global development of humanity. Commenting on the duty of the more fortunate peoples, the pope affirms that their obligations are rooted in a human and supernatural brotherhood. They present themselves under the threefold aspect of solidarity, social justice, and universal love, and their ultimate goal is 'to bring about a more human world for everyone, a world in which everyone will have something to give and something to receive, without the progress of one part constituting an obstacle to the development of the other'. The pope concludes the passage by saying that 'the problem is grave, since the future of the whole of civilisation depends on its solution'.

Without fear of repeating himself, Paul VI returns to what he calls 'the most urgent duty' (48) of the developed peoples, and insists that 'no nation can claim exclusive use of the wealth at its disposal' and that 'every nation must increase and improve its production, so that on the one hand it may give a truly human level of life to its people, and on the other, it may at the same time contribute to the global development of humanity'.

Guided by the masterly teaching of this encyclical which expresses the anguish of Paul VI, we shall consider this evening three possibilities of dialogue, capable, each from its own viewpoint, of taking a decisive step towards that universal solidarity which seems to have inspired *Populorum Progressio*. Humanity would have everything to gain by applying itself to the following threefold encounter:

(a) the encounter between christian and socialist worlds;

(b) the encounter between developed and underdeveloped worlds;

(c) the encounter between all religions, with the goal of a definitive initiative.

I. Encounter between christian and socialist worlds

When the Greco-Latin world, after three centuries of persecution, became to a great extent christian, and when the christians emerged from the catacombs to the dangerous splendour of the basilica and the imperial court, fears gained ground and were expressed with increasing intensity about the 'barbarians' who were arriving on the scene. It expresses all the Greco-Roman superiority and at the same time the fear of an impending collapse of the civilisation which seemed invincible.

The clearest symptom of this was seen in the great St Augustine, in anguish towards the end of his life, and verging on a state of panic for fear of the 'barbarians'. For all his genius, he failed to perceive the real significance of contemporary events, which, though they seemed catastrophic, were really only the beginning of a new world.

This historical episode comes to mind almost as a parallel to the attitude of European countries towards the socialist world. By European countries I mean the liberal capitalist or neo-capitalist world, but also the world which can be defined as 'christian'.

The socialist world is an easy target for European attacks. It accepts a marxist philosophy which is, or seemed to be, synonymous with materialism, and attacks religion which it considers to be the most powerful force for alienation. Atheism in the USSR has become militant, aggressive and official. The iron curtain made it easy to speak of the humiliation of the human person, of continual denunciation, of terrorism; rebellions have been drowned in blood and a wall of shame continues to stand in Berlin. But when red China appeared on the horizon there was almost an acceptance of Russia as a stabilising influence.

It is difficult to explode some of the myths which have been created and spread abroad by the European countries. Anti-communism is taught as the crusade of our times. The USSR is considered the number one enemy of freedom, of democracy, of christian civilisation; the enemy of God, of one's country and of the family. In the minds of many, the Russians have taken the place of horror and contempt once reserved for the Jews, as the deicide people. More recently, however, for some people, Russia has become enemy number two, red China having excelled the Soviet Union in its determination to dominate and destroy.

As the rival to the USSR and China, we have the United States of America, champion of christian civilisation, of democracy and of liberty. Many regard the US as the new chosen people, after twice saving the world. Many see it as the restorer of the European economy after the second world war and the driving force behind the development of the Third World. Many confer on it, with gratitude, the right and the duty to interfere whenever there is a danger of communism, and they consider just and providential any economic or even military measures taken to prevent it from spreading. Many find acceptable whatever type of war is waged by the United States, and they can find motives in their consciences to justify the escalation of war even to the point of a new Hiroshima and Nagasaki, if this were unavoidable.

With this mentality we can only widen the gap between the socialist and the christian worlds. These myths will inevitably lead to a third world war, with unforeseeable consequences for humanity. With this vision of the world it will be impossible, in practice, for us to understand the necessity and the urgency of universal solidarity.

We must be objective and have the courage to acknowledge the errors of both sides:

(*a*) Liberal capitalism, as *Populorum Progressio* says, has its own materialist roots and is directly responsible for the international dictatorship of economic power.

(*b*) We must stimulate the efforts of those communist thinkers who do not consider marxism to be an untouchable system. They are opposed to catechisms like that of Stalin; they rebel against a dogmatic, monolithic marxism, and condemn all the atrocities committed against nations which sought their own development and manifested a desire for self-determination.

(*c*) Why can we not recognise that there is more than one type of socialism, and so liberate the term from a necessary bond with materialism? Socialism is not necessarily a system which destroys the human person or the community. It can mean 'a system at the service of the community and of man'.

Let us not be blinded by passion. We must not confuse conflict of economic interests with religious wars or ideological battles. One one side and on the other we have seen egoism, in the strict sense, towards the crying needs of the Third World. In the United Nations Assembly we saw the insensitivity of the USSR, equalled only by that of the USA, regarding commerce and development. On both sides there has been contempt for self-determination by the people; there has been military occupation; atrocities have been committed.

How long will Latin America accept the imposition of regarding Cuba, her sister, as excommunicate?

Those who rebelled in Cuba only wanted to save her from underdevelopment and misery, and initially they appealed for help to Canada and the United States. Whoever leaves a people without possibilities like that, is responsible for the errors committed as a result!

We are told that to draw close to Cuba is to expose Latin America to the terrible danger of being cubanised. Since when was democracy incapable of dialogue? Since when are we so ingenuous that we do not know that to isolate Cuba, to castigate her for the crime of attempting self-determination—and we boast about respecting it—is to abandon her to the orbit of Soviet imperialism. And it has the unfortunate effect, especially among young people, of creating the myth of Cuba, the model of revolution and of underdevelopment conquered.

At Expo '67 in Canada, you can see, side by side, the pavilions of the capitalist and socialist countries. If you visit them, without prejudice, you will see that both worlds achieve the same results: the same technological development which harmonises with love for the truth and for all that is noble and good; with love for children, for young people and for the family.

Why not throw from one world to the other the same bridge of concord which unites the USA and USSR pavilions at Montreal?

II. Encounter between developed and underdeveloped worlds

An effective encounter between East and West would foster dialogue between developed and underdeveloped worlds. What seems to be utopia would follow, perhaps in a short time, as the consequence of the blind alley which the world has reached regarding war. No-one is so crazy as to start a thermonuclear war, now that the nuclear bomb is not a monopoly of any country and that the consequences of radioactivity are well-known. Local war is becoming more expensive, in money and in human life, than a world war.

If we could destroy the myths directed against the socialist world, and if the socialist world, for their part, could exorcise themselves of the anti-capitalist myths, the effect would certainly lead to an end of the suicidal arms race, to a general prohibition on using the atom for war purposes, and to a real respect for the self-determination of nations.

The development of the Third World is tied up with the interests of the developed world. We are not dealing only with the escalation of misery and the explosion of underdevelopment.

The United States, pursuing a myopic and short-term policy, is anxious to avoid rapid and profound change in Latin America and to keep human masses in sub-human conditions, provided the social pseudo-order is preserved and its own internal security is not disturbed. But in the framework of an intelligent and long-term policy, the US is interested in a Latin America with purchasing power and inter-trade capacity. The same is true for Europe with regard to Africa, for the USSR, Japan and red China with regard to Asia.

When wars are ended, and the arms race is finished —and I insist that political realism will achieve this ideal of peace sooner than we think—the technology of developed regions will stimulate the birth and the expansion of technology in the underdeveloped countries, if only for the necessity of total employment of labour or the service of interests which go beyond the petty and immediate.

You think I am wandering or dreaming? If I am correct, this seeming fantasy arises from very real interests. At any rate, it is a joy to discover the realism of *Populorum Progressio*. We are closer than many imagine to a harmonious and united civilisation. Have I forgotten that egoism will accompany man to the end of time? That sin has entered the world and casts its diabolical shadow over it? I am hoping for a little respite. My generation has already witnessed two world wars and has reached the brink of a third. War has become even more crazy and absurd with the possibility of destroying cities and exterminating civil populations and wiping out the whole of humanity. And this is the destructive side of a power which can construct to the point of assuring every human creature of a human level of life.

What are we doing with the immense power of the press, of radio, television, the cinema, the theatre? What are we doing with the education centres run by the universities? Why do we not try to harness this great potential and put it to the service of justice, of peace, of universal solidarity?

III. Encounter between all religions

It would greatly assist the dialogue between socialist and capitalist worlds, and also between developed and underdeveloped worlds, and it would be a decisive step towards universal solidarity if there could be more, much more than mutual respect, sympathy and goodwill between all religions. The ideal would be a joint programme and planned action by all religions working together for justice and peace, for universal solidarity and for development.

The catholic church and the World Council of Churches are ripe for such an integration. But it is not enough to unite brothers in Christ. We must arrive at a similar alliance with all non-christian religions beginning with those which are essential not only to ending or averting war but also to conquering underdevelopment in Asia and in Africa—in other words, judaism, islam, buddhism, hinduism.

Marxists regard religion as the great alienated and alienating force. We should have the honesty to acknowledge that in our preoccupation with eternal life, we can easily forget terrestrial life; in our concern for the social order, we do not always notice that it is often synonymous, in the Third World, with injustice and stratified disorder; in our anxiety to avoid profound and violent change, we use and abuse prudence, and almost always we act as the brake rather than the accelerator. And to carry honesty to extremes, we should recognise that it is always a temptation for us, difficult to determine yet interfering with our judgment and our work, that the wealthy and the government contribute to our social works and even to worship itself.

I pray that the renewal which is at work in the catholicism of Vatican II will be accomplished in all religions. In reality, there is at least a desire to imitate Christ in his wish to serve and not to be served. And most important is the decision to be present in the world. Instead of sinning by omission, instead of making remote judgments and condemnations, and being a spectator, the church wants to become flesh, like Christ, to accept the joys and the hopes, the problems and the anxieties of men.

At the Mar del Plata[1] conference, our bishops were resolved to take an active part in the development and integration of Latin America. If in the past our preaching, catechesis and liturgy assisted conformism, consciously or otherwise, and prolonged the sub-human situation of the masses, the catholic church is preparing to adopt a new attitude deriving from a theology of development and capable of transforming itself in tremendous force for the development of the continent.

Christian philosophy of man leads us to urge man to regard himself as co-creator; to act as a subject of history rather than an object; to have confidence, to overcome apathy and fear, and to act as one with a mission from God to dominate nature and complete creation. For christians, the incarnation of Christ is a living lesson in commitment.

We cannot be satisfied with a catechetical renewal which resolves itself only in greater activity or acceptability. We want a catechesis which can discover in the divine message truths capable of helping the masses to become a people and of converting the rich, whose senses have been dulled by money.

We cannot be satisfied with a liturgical renewal which resolves itself merely in moving the altar or giving to the people a more active part in the singing or in the prayers. We want the liturgy to support and deepen our catechesis, exalting the humble and shaking the

[1] The 10th Extraordinary Assembly of the Latin American Episcopal Council which took place at Mar del Plata (Argentina) from 9 to 16 October 1966. Cf address given on that occasion by Dom Helder Camara, pp 112–30 below.

pride of the powerful. The refreshing breeze which blows through catholic circles should not make us forget what can and must be done by other religious groups.

If help is to be given on a world scale then all who have the responsibility of believing in God must give the example of mutual help and cooperation, over and above the ideal of human solidarity common to all religions.

My dream is that an invitation, arising from the Pontifical Commission *Justitia et Pax*, shall be extended to all unitive religious bodies like the World Council of Churches, and that each religion shall indicate, clearly and objectively, the truths of its teaching which are capable of overcoming egoism and promoting justice and peace, universal solidarity and the humanisation of the world. There should be place also for agnostics in such an open ecumenical encounter, and for atheists who are christians in practice, who seek the truth, who hunger and thirst for peace based on justice, in a world countersigned by love.

To some people, this conference may indicate premature and dangerous ideas. My suggestions for dialogue between the developed and underdeveloped world, and between all the religions of the world, can easily be accepted. What is more likely to give rise to misunderstanding and opposition is my concern for a closer bond between East and West and, above all, my allusion to Cuba. There are those who are more christian than the pope and for whom anti-communism is a political expedient and a way of life. They will not be slow to discover in my words a proof of communist tendencies and a service rendered, however unwittingly, to the cubanisation of our country—undoubtedly the underhand work of Fidel Castro.

Brazil must not be treated as if it were an intellectual backwater! It no longer has any sense to classify as subversive and communist those who long for justice and peace; who refuse to narrow their vision of the world to two possibilities, capitalism and communism, as if to repudiate capitalism and be at variance with the United States were synonymous with abandonment to Russia or China.

In any eventuality, allow me to introduce myself. I am a human creature who regards himself as brother of all men without exception. I am a christian who recognises that Jesus Christ died not only for christians but for all men without exception. I am a bishop who thanks God for the human qualities of John XXIII and Paul VI; a bishop who rejoices at *Populorum Progressio* and will be happy to suffer for universal solidarity; who longs for it not only in words and vague concern but in practice, through a rapprochement of all religions, of developed and underdeveloped, of East and West.

7
Dialogue between universities

Conference held at Cornell University, New York, on 9 February 1967.

I. Purpose of my visit

Peace in the world is constantly threatened and man is running the risk of eliminating life from the face of the earth. This is the reason for Paul VI's visit to the United Nations as a 'pilgrim of peace', and why he risks misunderstanding and censure over Vietnam. The time has come to bring together all the leaders—of religion, of politics, of industry, of work and of public opinion —in an attempt to save mankind.

Obviously therefore we must include the universities and institutes of higher education. I am visiting the universities of the United States in order to point out the decisive role which belongs to the universities of the world at this time. We want to encourage a dialogue on the problem of peace at a radical level, between the universities of the underdeveloped world, of Latin America, Asia and Africa, and the universities of the developed world.

But first let me bring to your attention the particular tasks of even greater importance which must take priority in the universities of the developed and under-developed countries. Believe me, I am not addressing you as a Brazilian nor even as a Latin American. I have come as a christian to speak to my brothers in Christ, as a man who shares with you the same heavenly Father and is therefore in every sense a brother.

II. Possibility and value of dialogue

(a) *Peace from a Third World point of view*   The universities of the Third World would do well to study peace from their own point of view, in preparing themselves for dialogue with North American and European universities. In order to have the moral force to invite the universities of the developed world to examine the existence of world-scale injustice in the relationship between the wealthy and the non-indus-trialised nations—the indissoluble bond between justice and peace is taken for granted—the universities of the Third World must cease functioning as ivory towers surrounded by misery. It is imperative for them to be integrated in the harsh reality of which they form a part.

It is vital that they become aware of the problems of the people around them; that they denounce the worst examples of internal colonialism (for instance, Brazilians whose wealth derives from the misery of other Brazilians); that they help the sub-human masses to become a people and prepare this people for de-velopment. If it is a question of helping the people to emerge from misery and sub-human conditions, it is not enough to teach them to read and write. The sub-human situation leaves profound impressions on human beings. The man who depends entirely on the property owner, who lives on his land in a miserable hut, receives a wretched wage which permits him to stave off starvation and wear rags for clothes, who can be sacked and dismissed without notice—such a man is incapable of a man-to-man or brother-to-brother relationship with his employer. He is rather in the position of a slave to his master.

A man who vegetates in such deplorable conditions without a minimum of education, or independence from his employer, tends to abandon all hope and to identify his religion with a sad fatalism: 'These things are ordained by God; some are born poor, some are born rich. We were born poor. It was written in the heavens.' They think and speak like that. Mere reading and writing will not solve problems of this dimension. Initiative must be aroused; leaders must be encouraged; group-work must be taught and they must learn not to wait for the government to do everything.

'Demystification'[1] is the term we have coined to express this work of opening the eyes of the people, of stimulating consciousness, of helping man to use his freedom and his conscience, helping man to become a man. It is strange that the propertied classes are opposed to all demystification of the masses. Even the government is alarmed at discovering that it is easier to open the eyes of the masses than to alter the structure

[1] There is no single English or Italian word to express exactly this idea of making a people aware of their situation. The author's *coscientizzazione* is here given its nearest English equivalent. [Tr]

of society. But whoever attempts to make them aware of their situation will be accused of subversion and communism.

It is easy to retort that their eyes will be opened with us or without us or against us. If this happened tomorrow, and the masses of Latin America had the impression that christianity was afraid, that it lacked the courage to speak out before the government and the propertied classes, they would reject christianity because in their eyes it would clearly be an ally of their exploiters.

The best way to combat marxism is to teach a religion which is not 'the opium of the people'; to preach a christianity which, in union with Christ and following his example, embodies and appropriates all human problems in order to accomplish man's redemption.

(*a*) *North American universities and peace*   There can be no doubt that there exists a dialogue between the North American universities. What I ask and desire is a dialogue on the root problems of peace. Allow me to suggest some points for an examination of conscience and to give my own impressions of the situation. But remember that I speak not as a stranger but as a human brother, and for many of you, a brother in Christ.

When the United States asks young people to go to war and, if necessary, to die in defence of the free world:

(i) To what point is this appeal based on an objective vision of reality?

(ii) To what point are other motives present, over and

above the defence of the so-called 'free world', and to what point are these motives valid?

(iii) To what point can North Americans do as they wish even to risking the extermination of humanity?

Let us examine each question in turn.

Is fighting and dying for the free world a realistic objective? If I am not deceived, the United States starts with the presupposition that communism is the greatest evil. No sacrifice is too great to prevent communism from crushing human lives, suppressing liberty, dividing families, destroying religion and trying to dispel the very idea of God. On these premisses, much money is spent, many lives are lost, yesterday in Korea, today in Vietnam and tomorrow wherever it may be necessary. It is not the point to say that the US also combats misery, sending food, clothing and medicine in large quantities to the famine areas. As we shall see, the problem is not one of assistance. For the present, however, let us just take note of the equivocation which includes famine areas in the 'free world'.

Are there other motives to be added to the supposed defence of the supposedly free world? We must be sincere with ourselves and with the young people whom we send out to fight and die. Is it human liberty which is being defended or is it a struggle to save the neo-capitalist world which the US embodies and represents?

Who is not aware, these days, that capitalism and socialism no longer exist in the singular? There are many variations of them and the two systems are correlative. Today the United States and Russia are in reality less far apart than is imagined by ingenuous anti-

76

communists, who tremble with horror before the hammer and sickle. No-one with the capacity to see the shape of future events would be surprised at an alliance between Russia and the US against China. To what point, under the pretext of combating ideologies, is there in reality conflicts of interest, a collision of empires? The atrocities committed in this battle and in this conflict are equal on both fronts.

III. Important event for world peace

(c) *Inter-university dialogue* It seems to me urgent to get under way a dialogue between the European and North American universities on the one hand, and the Latin American, African and Asiatic universities on the other, with a view to working out something together for world peace. To this end it is necessary to examine the manner in which relations are conducted between the developed and the underdeveloped worlds.

The Third World claims that an injustice on a world scale can clearly be established by comparing the capital invested in it by the industrialised countries with the profit extracted from it, and also by comparing the help received by the underdeveloped countries with the prices imposed on raw materials.

The problem therefore is not only that the help given by the United Nations to the Third World is insufficient. It is true that 1% of the gross national product is like a drop in the ocean. And it is also true that not even this 1% is reached by the entire United Nations (in 1961, total aid for underdeveloped countries reached 0·87%; in 1964 this total had already fallen to 0·66%). And unfortunately it is true that this help becomes ridiculous and meaningless when compared with expenditure on war. But a still graver problem is the claim of the underdeveloped countries that while minimal help is given with one hand, the other is working for their impoverishment.

Why don't the universities of the world study, at a university level, the data on commerce and development presented by the United Nations Assembly? If the Prébisch report was false, its errors and shortcomings should be denounced; if it was true, it is too serious a matter not to merit world attention. Who is not aware that peace is impossible without justice? Who is not aware that modern warfare is a danger for the whole of humanity?

On the recommendation of the second Vatican Council, Paul VI set up at Rome a secretariat for justice and peace in the world. This body, so aptly named, is of the greatest importance, indispensable, and could not have been postponed any longer. It shows that the pope understands clearly the lack of justice in the world, and that peace is a dream without justice.

Two men from the developed countries will occupy key-positions in the direction of the secretariat, two men who are deeply sensitive to the grave problems of the underdeveloped world: Cardinal Le Roy, a Canadian, and Mgr Gremillion, a North American.

May God grant that this secretariat for justice and peace in the world may be a sensitive radar for denouncing each and every injustice, wherever it may occur, independently of race, religion or ideology. May God grant that it may have the moral authority to contribute efficaciously to the salvation of peace by the salvation of justice. May God grant that the universities of the entire world may help the secretariat to function as the conscience of the free world.

8
Education for change

A conference given in English at Princeton University, USA, on 10 February 1967.

I. An important topic

I am grateful for your invitation to come here from Brazil to speak to you, and I have chosen for my subject a theme which will justify my journey and the time which you are kindly giving to me.

I want to talk to you about education as an instrument of change. But we must do more than make general observations and polite comments, after which each of us can go away contented and take up again the rhythm of our normal lives. And therefore I propose to talk to you not about transformation in general, but about the rapid and radical change which is necessary in the Third World, including Latin America. I want to remind you that a transformation of this nature—a social revolution—will be possible in the underdeveloped world only if the developed world has the humility to understand and to accept that social revolution in Africa, Asia and Latin America presupposes, of necessity, a social revolution in Europe and North America.

The question we must ask is whether this social revolution, which the whole world needs, can be achieved by education, or whether it will come about through violence and armed conflict. Certainly we shall not exhaust our subject, perhaps we shall not even reach agreement on this great problem.

II. Motives for social revolution

(a) *Need for rapid change*   Asia and Africa have been decolonised, especially after the second world war, and we have the spectacle in the United Nations of independent countries taking their place alongside the great powers like the USA and USSR.

But Latin America, with more than a century of experience, can demonstrate to her sisters in underdevelopment that political independence alone is far from sufficient. Political independence without economic independence is an illusion.

It is a serious matter that, while external colonialism is ended—at least in Latin America, and I suppose the same is true in Asia and Africa—the worst form of colonialism continues. I mean internal colonialism, Brazilians who are enriched by the poverty of other Brazilians, and this happens in most of the countries of Latin America.

It cannot be easy for you to understand what I call 'internal colonialism'. Let me remind you that for three centuries—and for part of the nineteenth century—we in Latin America received into our countries millions of Africans whom we enslaved, as did also the United States. And we accommodated our christian consciences to this reality. When we abolished the slavery of Africans, we carried on with a type of national slavery, though without giving it that name. This can be described as follows: The worker can live on his master's land; he receives a house for himself, his wife and his children, his work is assured by his master's property and almost always he will be given a plot of land of his own. Thus the property-owner considers himself, in his heart, to be a real father, kindly and generous. And if the worker's hut seldom has water or light or toilet facilities, the master excuses himself by saying: 'God gives according to our needs.' (Who will deliver us from this image of a God who is really the fruit of our own self-centredness? We need to assume our responsibility as co-creators, as subjects of history who guide the course of earthly events.)

The master is convinced that he has the right to decide how he shall pay his employee; in fact, has he not already condescended to give him work and a house and a little plot of his own? If the worker shows any ingratitude, if he makes claims to being a human person, busies himself with new ideas, attends one of the 'radio' schools, enrols in a trade union, talks about rights, then the owner will be convinced that these alarming symptoms are a prelude to revolt, even communism itself, who knows? And almost certainly he will dismiss the worker from his land, if necessary breaking down the hut which houses his wife and family.

The master, a christian, has not even the slightest suspicion that he is violating one of the fundamental human rights enumerated by John XXIII: the right to existence and to a dignified standard of living; economic rights, especially the right to human work which is healthy, creative, free, which gives him a fair wage and makes possible private property; the right to culture and therefore to basic education (the minimal part of those rights which relate to moral and cultural values); the right to associate with others and to attend meetings; the right to honour God according to the dictates of informed conscience. And if the worker is unjustly treated by one who believes in God the creator and Father, and if he finds connivance on the part of the church which continually affirms that we are all brothers, all children of the same heavenly Father, how can this disillusioned man praise and honour God with peace of spirit and serenity of mind?

If you think I am exaggerating, ask the Peace Volunteers, who have just returned from Latin America, Africa and Asia, if the condition of these masses, who do not merit the name 'people', is indeed sub-human. Ask them to describe the slums they live in, the disease, the malnutrition, the lack of a minimum of educational conditions and freedom of work.

These sub-human situations have terrible consequences: this creature feels a slave before his almighty master, he feels an innate incapacity, and his religion is identified with the most desperate fatalism. God appears to permit and approve that some should have everything and others nothing.

The owners, naturally, think that they are doing everything humanly possible for their employees. They themselves are waiting for development so that, with the industrialisation of their plantations, they can have the necessary resources to raise the living standards of their workers. But experience has shown that with industrialisation the rich get richer and the poor, apart from the small number of those who find work, get even poorer, while the destitute sink still deeper into sub-human conditions.

But there are some young people who are despairing of the peaceful methods of persuasion adopted by reformers to achieve human living conditions for their brothers vegetating on their land. They maintain that the owners will never permit any attempt to promote the human advancement of these sons of God, to awaken their initiative, to raise up leaders, to teach them to work together, to stimulate their numbed intellects and their sense of freedom, to make them aware.

Experience teaches us, and there is no denying it, that basic education and popular culture does awaken the consciousness of human beings. We know how to help the masses to become a people and how to prepare the people for development. What we are not sure of is whether education removes the blinkers from the eyes of the rich, pierces the armour of selfishness, changes ideas and conscience and really leads to reform of economico-social structures.

Before replying and, I hope, provoking thought and discussion, I should like to examine why Europe and North America have need of a social revolution and why we shall strive in vain for rapid and radical transformation of the Third World without a similar transformation of the developed countries.

(b) *The need for change in developed countries* The idea that Europe and North America have need of a social revolution must be strange for a European or

North American. Everything in your respective societies seems so secure and prosperous that you can only smile at the fantasy of the underdeveloped world which attributes to you the problems of destitution.

Let us take a look at your country, however, where, if I am not mistaken, a social revolution is at present going on in three areas, each originating from a different source and leading to diverse results: the struggle of the Negroes for racial integration; the struggle for social advancement of 30 million Americans who are destitute in the richest country of the world; and the war against war.

The struggle for racial integration is surely one of the noblest pages in the recent history of your country. But although it has brought to light outstanding christian leaders like Dr Martin Luther King, and although it has made some progress and found many adherents even in the government itself, it will continue, in a general way, to be an arduous struggle which will demand great sacrifice and heroism on the part of our Negro brothers. How blind we become when passion enters into our conflicts! The United States is aware that this is a most vulnerable point on which it can lose moral force. How can you talk of democracy and present yourself to the world as the champion of liberty while the Negroes, who may have equal legal status, are segregated in practice?

The fight against poverty has been proclaimed by your president Lyndon Johnson. The world has admired his unflinching courage in acknowledging the presence in this country of 30 million people in conditions which are incompatible with human dignity. It is the hope of the underdeveloped world that when the problem of integrating these 30 millions into the full life of the country has been tackled and solved, this American potential will be thrown wholeheartedly into the fight against world poverty, into the struggle for a civilisation in harmony and solidarity.

If I am not mistaken, there have not as yet been any decisive victories in the war against poverty in the US. The root of the trouble lies, perhaps, in the American bias in favour of the arms race, and in the local wars which could, at any moment, degenerate into a world war. As long as communism appears to be the greatest of all evils; as long as the average American persists in the illusion that to die in Korea or in Vietnam is to die for the free world—an illusion because two-thirds of humanity do not belong to this free world, living as they do in destitution and sub-human conditions, and being slaves to hunger, disease, ignorance and internal colonialism; as long as the American middle class fails to understand that there are many types of socialism and many types of capitalism, to the point that Russia and the US are less far apart than many ingenuous anti-communists think; as long as the American middle class is incapable of realising that the gravest social problem of our time is the ever-widening gap between the rich who get richer and the poor who get poorer; as long as there is no change of mentality, no revolution of ideas, the United States will be unequal to its immense responsibility of being the greatest democracy of our time.

From here, the war against war develops and expands to embrace the youth of the world. When will humanity realise the barbarity of a criterion of right which is based on the greater or lesser capacity to destroy? How long will the US, under the pretext of defending the human person, permit thousands of bombers to drop bombs in immense quantities over open cities, striking down women and children and the sick? How long will this great country contain those who can defend a repetition of Hiroshima and Nagasaki?

III. Education or violence?

You may well ask whether I regard education as a viable means of changing socio-economic structures in the underdeveloped world and of making the developed countries understand that they too are in need of a social revolution.

With respect to those who despair of education and appeal to violence, I do not believe in hatred. The problem does not consist in changing some leaders and enforcing a transformation which, by peaceful means, would be postponed or remain at the planning stage or not even be understood. Violence cannot plant roots, it doesn't change mentalities. If what is done by force is not understood by the losing party, it begets bitterness and resentment; if it is not understood by the beneficiary it will be reduced to nothing for lack of internal preparation in the rightful use of what has been gained.

I cherish a dream, which is difficult to realise but, if I am correct, is capable of bringing about rapid and radical change and a creative revolution. If the universities concern themselves with the problems which we have discussed, if they accept them as valid and use all the moral force at their disposal, we shall have taken the first step towards education for change.

If we spiritual leaders of all religions, christian and

non-christian, collaborate with agnostics and atheists in a sincere search for truth, we shall have enormous moral authority to examine the relation between the developed and underdeveloped worlds. As long as there is question of justice on a world scale, the peace of the world will be in the balance.

We christians are far from exhausting the riches contained in the truths we teach. If we are convinced that we are all brothers, children of the same heavenly Father; that it is God's will that we should cooperate in and complete the work of creation and dominate nature; that it is the church's task to continue Christ, to be made flesh like the word of God who dwelt among us—if we really believe this, we shall have an immeasurable force to turn to the benefit of world unity and to the earthly redemption of man, the sign and pledge of his eternal redemption.

If to the work of the universities and the spiritual leaders we join in the power of the press, the collaboration of labour leaders and heads of commerce, and the participation of political and military leaders, we shall be in a position, I believe, to give decisive proof of the power of education and of the value of the democratic system.

The pessimist will say that none of these forces are free; that the universities are tied to the state or to the rigid schemes of their foundations; that the spiritual leaders, enjoying the help of rich and influential friends, are prisoners of a subtle power which is greater than they imagine; that the reviews, the newspapers, radio and television are becoming great undertakings, making it impossible for writers to be free, since their liberty ends where the commercial interests of the great organisations begin; that the businessmen, though personally human and christian, are caught in the system and imprisoned in the commercial machine; that the workers in underdeveloped areas have no freedom, since they are tied to their sub-human work and are without effective guarantees; that the workers in developed areas, in proportion as their economic situation improves, lose their revolutionary impetus; that political leaders are subject to their parties and the military to their codes and discipline.

It is said that Abraham hoped against hope. I hope not only in the help of God who will not abandon to destruction the chief work of creation, but also in man's intelligence and good sense. Selfishness will no longer have place among us when all can perceive and understand that man has the potential to destroy humanity or to ensure for all an adequate level of well-being.

The human instinct of preservation will continue to function. May we christians be examples of egoism overcome in our day, models of largeness of heart, of brotherly understanding which transcends difference of faith, of race and of religion! May we christians be worthy of the responsibility and honour of bearing the name of Christ!

9
Recife and Milan, sisters and allies

Lecture given on 27 May 1967, in the auditorium of the PIME *Missionary Centre, Milan, at an exhibition held to celebrate the publication of the encyclical* Populorum Progressio.

In this evening's lecture I should like to suggest why, in my opinion, Recife and Milan have a great responsibility in the common effort of the world to translate the encyclical *Populorum Progressio* into practice. I think I am correct in saying that my own city Recife, for very serious reasons, needs to make great efforts in the heart of the underdeveloped world comparable only to what is expected, in the heart of the developed world, by your city Milan. Do not think this comparison is presumptuous and arrogant. It expresses rather my feeling for the city of St Ambrose and St Charles Borromeo, for the archdiocese led today with wisdom by Cardinal Colombo, and still imbued with the spirit of Cardinal Montini.

It is my firm hope that the dialogue between our two cities may grow and intensify, so that we shall never lose sight of one another, so that we may stimulate one another and work together in harmony and concord. And let us make a spiritual pact to leave to providence the measurement of our efforts, and let providence judge the evidence by the light of *Populorum Progressio*.

I. The responsibility of Recife

Latin America–Brazil–Recife   I am convinced that Latin America has greater responsibility than Asia and Africa within the Third World since, for more than a century, all the Latin American countries have enjoyed political independence, and all the more since the entire continent is christian.

Note that I am not talking about prestige or superiority, but about responsibility, in other words the obligation to bear witness, to respond to what has been given. And in this respect, Latin America has been more fortunate than the other two underdeveloped continents.

Still on the subject of responsibility, it is easy to see that Brazil bears the heaviest responsibility in Latin America, since, on grounds of territory and population, it covers more than a third of the whole continent. Within Brazil, the greatest responsibility falls on the North-East and on Recife its capital, because this region, more than any other in Latin America, is experiencing planned development at its most rational and consistent.

Recife itself   What is the duty of a bishop who arrives in a city to find that two-thirds of the people entrusted to him by God are living in a sub-human situation?

What is his first obligation as a man, as a christian, as a father, as a shepherd? Without losing any time, he must help his people to achieve a human level of life.

When the dwellings are infected slums, unfit to be called houses, often surrounded by filth; when the work is degrading, without guarantees, with a wage so insecure as to provide only a precarious level of nutrition and an inhuman life; when the minimal conditions for educating children and developing an authentic christian life are wanting, then the words of the pope's encyclical are brought into sharp relief: 'It is not sufficient to struggle against destitution however urgent and necessary this may be,' but we must strive 'to ensure a fully human life for all men, one which is free from slavery imposed by men or by uncontrolled nature: a world in which liberty is not an empty word'.

These words of your former archbishop, who is now the pope, deserve closer study. You will have understood clearly his ideas: untamed nature is a slavery, and there are other forms of slavery which proceed from man. Situations exist in the world, and particularly in the Brazilian North-East and in Recife, in which liberty, God's noblest gift to man in the natural order, has lost its meaning. For anyone who lives at a sub-human level it remains an empty word.

The idea of controlling nature is something that has not yet been grasped by the great mass of Latin Americans, who do not realise that God the creator has made man his co-creator, giving him the right and imposing on him the duty of conquering nature and completing creation. We must bring about this awareness in the masses of Recife, of Brazil, of Latin

America, of the whole Third World. Throughout the underdeveloped world you can see the legacy of age-long destitution: the sense of dejection, of impotence, of sadness. Religion, for these people, has become fatalism. If it rains too much, you must pray that it will stop; if it does not rain enough, you must pray that it soon will. Certainly we must pray, but it is also necessary to cooperate with God's help, not just to pray and leave it at that!

And so we come to another consequence of enduring destitution: inequality and social injustice are regarded as inevitable and attributed to the will of God. Some are born rich, some are born poor; it is useless doing anything about it, these things will never change anyway. These sentiments are by no means christian. The christian knows that he must change the course of nature and work for greater social justice. The underdeveloped masses must be made to understand this.

We Latin Americans, we Brazilians, must lift the burden of slavery which we lay on the shoulders of our brothers. In order to have the right to speak to the world about development, we must have the courage to denounce also our own sins against justice and against the law of love; let us clean up our own house, before looking at the dirt in our neighbour's!

The developed nations, who defend 'the free world' or 'the liberty of the world' by going to war in under-developed lands, with the ideal of liberating them from the slavery of communism, should learn from Paul VI that poverty also is a slavery, and that freedom is an empty word for two-thirds of humanity. I said this a short time ago in America. I have come to Italy after giving conferences in four American universities and I never tired of repeating: you Americans believe in freedom because you enjoy it, but take note, the word 'liberty' is absolutely meaningless for the greater part of mankind, in the underdeveloped countries!

Recife and the North-East The North-East, while retaining all the characteristics of an underdeveloped region, is the area of Brazil which has evolved economically with the greatest rapidity in the last six years, thanks mainly to heavy investment in electric power, roads and general improvement of the basic conditions for higher production, and thanks also to a decisive industrialisation policy stimulated by generous fiscal assistance.

The Catholic Workers' Action (ACO) recently denounced this development as unjust and inhuman.[1] Antiquated industries, especially textiles and sugar refineries, are being modernised by the Centre for the Development of north-east Brazil (SUDENE), which is stimulating the expansion of industry equipped from the outset with modern machinery. Now, the more modern the undertaking, the more it is automated, and the less need it has of manual labour. The result, in the underdeveloped countries, is a tragic problem of unemployment and an enormous gap between well-to-do workers and the great mass of destitute.

The situation is different in an industrialised country, where, for example, coal mines may have to close because they cannot compete with countries which can extract better coal in a more economical way. But advanced technology will permit this country to con-

[1] See pp 131–181 below.

tinue using its coal for some other purpose, its flourishing economy will enable it to create new industries, its skilled workers will have the possibility of rapid integration into other work.

You can imagine what happens when the technology is not advanced, when the economy is not flourishing, when the workers have not the cultural capacity of learning a new trade! The direction of development is almost as important as development itself. Development alone is insufficient; it must be human and respect the interests of the disinherited masses.

This, then, is the great task which faces Recife: to spur on the North-East to a truly human development which will take account of all the people of the region. We must engage our universities in the study of the problems at a scientific level, examining the experiences of others and creating new outlets for work. We must ensure the finance for solving our problems by convincing the wealthy of our region to resist the temptation of higher profits, of accumulating their capital in Swiss banks and of shirking expenditure in a manner which is often a scandal and an affront to destitution. Let us stimulate the awareness and the potential of the poor, that they may take an active part, by their work and their professional qualification, in their own development.

Recife in relation to Brazil The Brazilian North-East knows from experience that it will not be developed without the fraternal help of the developed areas of our country. In Brazil, it was the South which developed rapidly, and in particular São Paolo, the 'Milan of Brazil'. Milan understands very well its own responsibility for integrating into development the less developed areas of Italy and recognises that no country can be truly developed if it keeps some of its regions at the margin of progress. Recife is constantly trying to convince the South that the North-East, while needing the collaboration of the South for its development, will in time provide a most important market for the southern industries.

Recife is doing everything possible to initiate a dialogue between the Brazilian North-East and the South; a dialogue between the universities, the newspapers, the trade unions, radio and television; a dialogue also through the personal contacts of industrial leaders, politicians, in short, between all the principal channels. And it is logical that such a dialogue should look confidently to the church for her presence and support, not in terms of dominion and control, but in the terms and in the spirit of service.

Latin America and Recife   Nothing opens the eyes and clears the mind like suffering and poverty. The North-East, struggling for development and needing the collaboration of the South to integrate itself into the rest of the country, understands, desires and demands that Brazil should take its place generously in the Latin American endeavour for integration.

No Latin-American country is capable alone of tackling the great economic blocs which claim to divide up the world. Either there is mutual and fraternal collaboration or the continent will not be redeemed from underdevelopment. Precisely because it is undergoing this experience, at its own expense, the North-East is in a position to give some extremely important advice to Latin America. It insists that the Latin American Common Market will achieve nothing if it remains the satellite of a foreign economic power, and that it will be ineffectual if only one of the member countries—and especially one of the bigger countries—repeats, at the expense of its smaller neighbours, the economic imperialism which is causing us immense moral and material damage, and will continue to do so for a long time.

II. Milan and the developed world

Italy and Milan   At the heart of the developed world, Italy has a position of great responsibility, for it contains within its territory the seat of the vicar of Christ. This responsibility is even greater since providence has sent to catholics and to all men of goodwill a prophet like John XXIII and, as his successor, Pope Paul VI, clear-sighted and far-seeing, expert in humanity and pilgrim of peace.

If for these reasons Italy has a great responsibility before God, we must not forget that Milan is the capital of Italian development, the capital of the famous 'industrial triangle' which comprises also Turin and Genoa. Allow me therefore, in the name of Recife, to enter for a few moments into dialogue with your city.

Milan and Italian integration   I shall not dare to pretend to a deep knowledge of Milan, since I know well that to know the heart of a city it is not even sufficient to be born and to live one's life in it. But it is possible to feel the pulse of a city. And I know that Milan is winning the battle against egoism. I am convinced that your city preserves its humanity, while still being one of the great metropolises of the world. Milan offers house, work and security to the emigrants from other regions of Italy, gives a professional qualification to all who settle within its boundaries, creates human conditions of life for those who come to it in great number and in great need. Most admirable has been the attention which has been lavished on absorbing internal immigration with a fraternal spirit, and on avoiding ghettos, always unpleasant and inhuman.

Above all Milan is recognising that the help it offers for the development of southern Italy turns to its own honour and advantage, because with this attitude your city gives proof of intelligence, of using the head as well as the heart. Thus there is a similarity between Milan and São Paolo. Any difference there may be consists in the fact that the developed region of Italy is the North, while in Brazil it is the South.

Certainly it is important that Milan should develop; but this expansion should not be merely economic, since it is necessary to lend a helping hand to the total Italian effort for completing the political integration of the country with the urgent and indispensable economic and spiritual integration. The Third World looks to Milan to help Italy achieve a self-awakening in the heart of the underdeveloped world, an awareness of two of the greatest problems of our time, brought into striking relief by *Populorum Progressio.*

Milan's role in the world   When the pope makes a decision, he knows what he is doing and why he is doing it. When he created the Pontifical Commission for Justice and Peace—whose name is itself a programme—he let it be understood that he was absolutely convinced that relations in the developed and underdeveloped worlds cannot be reduced to assistance. There are world-scale problems of justice to be solved and without justice there cannot be peace among men. But an underdeveloped country appears to be ungrateful if it echoes the words of the pope, if it upholds the celebrated slogan 'trade not aid'.

Milan will be truly a sister to the developing peoples if it encourages Italy to take up the cause of justice and peace. Two things are essential: firstly, to examine honestly the relationship which exists between the help given to the poor countries by the rich and the total loss suffered by the same poor countries as a consequence of the iniquitous prices imposed on raw materials by the international market; secondly, to denounce the wicked disproportion which exists between the amount of money invested by the rich countries in the underdeveloped and the scandalously higher amount extracted by the rich from their investments.

This would be a practical application of *Populorum Progressio*. Milan is a practical city; it lives on the ground and is not content with empty words. It must implement the encyclical of Paul VI in such manner as to lead the developed world and make it aware of the injustices committed against the poor of the whole world.

Every now and then someone makes a discovery. The complex problem of underdevelopment is really only a simple question of the limitation of births! It seems that world poverty will be defeated when women, the mothers of the underdeveloped countries, are sterilised *en masse*. Milan must remind the brethren in developed countries that the battle against under-development can only be won by profound reforms in international commerce, in agriculture, in industry, in finance, in labour.

Milan, Milan! Consider as your own the Pontifical Commission for Justice and Peace, born of the intelligence and heart of your Cardinal Montini, Pope Paul VI.

Milan and the International Trusts   In some circles, *Populorum Progressio* has given rise to considerable anger and scorn, to the point of calling it *Populorum Regressio*, and this is due to the courage of Paul VI. It was already a step in the right direction to go beyond the concept of assistance and arrive at the notion of justice and peace. Paul VI goes even further and denounces in strong terms the international dictatorship of economic power.

How long will governments—and I am not talking of the governments of poor countries but of the powerful who take part in the arms race—how long will they allow international trusts to manipulate the world? It is quite striking: in any industrial country, the informed observer can easily discover that the hundreds and thousands of industrial and financial concerns can be reduced to about a dozen, an economic nucleus of almost unlimited power. And, from country to country, from continent to continent, these economic power blocs join forces, unite and work together. They are the lords of the world, the cold and despotic calculators of peace and war (and especially of war!).

As you probably know, the United States has regarded it a matter of national concern to face up to the trusts and to bring in suitable legislation to control their economic power, which could suffocate a great nation. It is worth reading the evidence of Senator Kefauver, president for many years of the senate subcommittee on trusts: this courageous and authoritative document demonstrates the spirit of the American people and the incredible power of the economic trusts which it needs a national effort to control. Why cannot we encourage the United Nations to extend the anti-trust laws and apply them at a world level? Italy and America have adopted them for their own internal use. Their extension to other countries would provide a fitting mission for Italy and for the city of Milan.

Who knows if my dream of a dialogue with Milan and with Italy will find an echo in the heart of your city and your country? My friends, I hope that divine providence will accomplish this dialogue, and that all of us together, inspired by *Populorum Progressio* and with the help of God, may work for the construction of a better future for the whole of humanity.

10
Violence—the only way?

A lecture given in Paris on 25 April 1968.

The subject is certainly topical. It is true that violence belongs to all ages, but today it is perhaps more topical than ever; it is omnipresent, in every conceivable form: brutal, overt, subtle, insidious, underhand, blind, rational, scientific, solidly entrenched, anonymous, abstract, irresponsible.

It isn't difficult to speak of violence if it is either to condemn it out of hand, from afar, without bothering to examine its various aspects or seek its brutal, and regrettable, causes; or if it is to fan the flames from a safe distance, in the manner of an 'armchair Che Guevara'.

What is difficult is to speak of violence from the thick of the battle, when one realises that often some of the most generous and the most able of one's friends are tempted by violence, or have already succumbed to it. I ask you to hear me as one who lives in a continent whose climate is pre-revolutionary, but who, while he has no right to betray the Latin American masses, has not the right either to sin against the light or against love.

Here is a first basic remark, necessary to the understanding of the problematic of violence: the whole world is in need of a structural revolution. With regard to the underdeveloped countries, this fact is self-evident. From whatever standpoint one approaches the question—economic, scientific, political, social, religious—it soon becomes obvious that a summary, superficial reform is absolutely insufficient. What is needed is a reform in depth, a profound and rapid change; what we must achieve—let's not be afraid of the word—is a structural revolution.

As Paul VI has recently said:

> One thing is certain, the present situation must be faced courageously, and the injustice it comprises must be fought and overcome. Audacious transformations and a profound renewal are the price of development. Reforms must be urgently undertaken, without delay. Everyone must generously play his part.

Economically speaking, it is common knowledge that the underdeveloped countries suffer from internal colonialism. A small group of rich and powerful people in each country maintains its power and wealth at the expense of the misery of millions of the population. This regime is still semi-feudal, with a semblance of a 'patriarchal' system, but in reality a total absence of personal rights; the situation is sub-human, the conditions those of slavery. The rural workers, who are nothing more than pariahs, are denied access to the greater part of the land, which lies idle in the hands of rich landowners who are waiting for its value to rise.

With such a situation in a continent like Latin America, which is wholly christian—at least in name and tradition—one realises the great responsibility borne by christianity in such countries. Without forgetting the fine examples of devotion, of sacrifice, of heroism even, we must admit that in the past—and the danger still persists—we christians in Latin America have been, and are, seriously responsible for the situation of injustice which exists in this continent. We have condoned the slavery of Indians and Africans; and now are we taking a sufficiently strong stand against the landowners, the rich and the powerful in our own countries? Or do we close our eyes and help to pacify their consciences, once they have camouflaged their terrible injustice by giving alms in order to build churches (very often scandalously vast and rich, in shocking contrast with the surrounding poverty), or by contributing to our social projects? In practice, don't we seem to have vindicated Marx, by offering to pariahs a passive christianity, alienated and alienating, justly called an opium for the masses?

And yet christianity exists, with its demands of justice and fraternity; christianity exists, with its message of eternal redemption. Indeed, our love for mankind is inspired from within by a love which is greater than the dimensions of the world and which provides it with a radically new element. In this way christianity too is a motive force working for an integral development—including economic development—for scripture teaches that God gave man his image and likeness and wished him to subdue nature and bring creation to perfection.

If we Latin-American christians assume our responsibility in face of the underdevelopment of the continent we can and must work to promote radical changes in all sectors of social life, particularly in politics and education. Politics must not remain the preserve of a privileged few, who stand in the way of basic reforms by betraying them or agreeing to them on paper only. Education is so far below the needs of technology—itself in constant evolution—that the unrest of our students is easy to understand. They have no time for the superficial, timid, and empty university reforms that are imposed upon them.

My remarks about Latin America can, more or less, be transposed to the whole of the underdeveloped world, which is in crying need of a structural revolution.

It is harder to understand that the developed countries are also in need of a structural revolution. Isn't their advanced state of development a proof that they have achieved success? Why should they need a revolution? Let us glance for a moment at the two most successful forms of development, under the capitalist and socialist regimes, as exemplified by the United States and the Soviet Union.

The United States is a living demonstration of the internal contradiction of the capitalist system: it has succeeded in creating underdeveloped strata within the richest country in the world—30 million Americans live in a situation below the dignity of the human condition: it has succeeded in provoking a fratricidal war between whites and blacks; under the guise of anti-communism, but in fact driven by a lust for prestige and the expansion of its sphere of influence, it is waging the most shameful war the world has ever known. The dominant system in the United States is so irrational in its rationalisation, as they call it, that it has succeeded in creating a one-dimensional, 'robot' existence, to such an extent that young Americans of different cultural traditions feel called to build a more just and more human society by transforming the social context and humanising technology.

The Soviet Union considers itself motivated solely by scientific humanism, since it takes its inspiration from marxism. In practice, however, under the pretext of defending itself from the contamination of capitalism it perpetuates the iron curtain and the wall of shame; it refuses all pluralism within the socialist camp—the Soviet Union and red China face each other like two capitalist powers; and it considers marxism to be an untouchable dogma.

Marx failed to distinguish between the essence of christianity and the weakness of christians who, in practice, often reduced it to an opium for the people. But today there is a change of attitude among christians. Now, even in practice, there is an effort to preach and live a christianity that is by no means an alienated or alienating force, but that is incarnated among men, following the example of Christ. This change has not yet been understood by the Soviet Union.

The Soviet Union and the United States have just furnished yet one more example of their bad faith and incomprehension of the Third World, at New Delhi.

It is in vain that Asia at Bangkok, Africa at Algiers, and Latin America at Tequendama, in vain that the Third World in its letter from Algiers continues to repeat that the problems which vitiate relations between rich and poor countries are not a question of aid, but of *justice* on a world scale.

The two 'super-powers', supreme examples of capitalism and socialism, remain blind and deaf, enclosed and imprisoned in their egoism. How can the developed world be prevented from leaving the underdeveloped world each day further and further behind? Today, 85%, tomorrow 90%, rot in misery in order to make possible the excessive comfort of 15%, tomorrow 10%, of the world's population. Who can now fail to understand the need for a structural revolution in the developed world?

Before asking whether the structural revolution needed by the world necessarily supposes violence, it must be underlined that violence already exists and that it is wielded, sometimes unconsciously, by the very people who denounce it as a scourge of society.

It exists in the underdeveloped countries: the masses in a sub-human situation are exploited violently by privileged and powerful groups. It is well known that if the masses attempt to unite by means of education at grass roots level based on the popular culture, if they form trade unions or cooperatives, their leaders are accused of treason or communism. This has aptly been described as follows: 'they rebel against the established disorder, so they are classed as outlaws ... They must disappear so that order may reign.' An orderly disorder!

As for 'law', it is all too often an instrument of violence against the weak, or else it is relegated to the fine phrases of documents and declarations, such as the

Declaration of the Rights of Man, whose second decade the world is commemorating this year. A good way of celebrating this anniversary would be for the United Nations Organisation to verify if one or two of these rights are in fact respected in two-thirds of the world.

Violence also exists in the developed world, whether capitalist or socialist. In this respect, there are certain disquieting signs which speak for themselves. Negroes pass from non-violence to violence. The black apostle of non-violence is felled to the consternation and shame of all men of goodwill. We are filled with horror when we see, on the one hand, young Americans forced to raze whole regions by means of 'overkill', supposedly in order to protect the free world (we know the real reason); and on the other hand young men, children almost, obliged to kill in order to defend their lives, or rather sub-human existence. The youth of Western Germany, of Italy, of Spain, of Poland rise simultaneously in revolt. There is also the unique protest movement of the hippies. The arms race continues, and risks contaminating the space race. How splendid would be this glorious achievement of our age if the cosmonauts were not instruments of belligerence, of political and military prestige. Faced with the new Czechoslovakia, the Soviet Union's uneasiness is evident and, under the pretext of safeguarding the unity of the socialist camp, it rekindles the ideological battle against the capitalist world.

Here are a few more glimpses of our present world:

(a) The pound sterling, once so solid, is forced to devalue and the ancient queen of the seas may be forced to abandon her splendid isolation to become a part of the continent.

(b) The dollar is a cause of concern for dear old Uncle Sam, even though his economic situation is still as strong as ever.

(c) Automation troubles many people, and massive unemployment remains a nightmare, even in highly industrialised countries where re-employment would seem easy.

(d) National and international trusts are already more powerful than the most powerful states, and they manage to shield the gangsters they hire to eliminate certain personalities who are judged too much of a nuisance. It can be said that these trusts are the real 'lords of the world': it is they who are responsible for revolutions and wars.

It is easy to add to this list of what I have called 'disquieting signs', which are also signs of violence, more or less disguised, existing both in the capitalist and socialist worlds. Even more scandalous is the violence perpetrated by the developed world against the underdeveloped countries, as we have already seen in connection with the failure of the Second UNCTAD Conference at New Delhi.

Faced with this triple violence—that which exists in the Third World, or in the developed world, or that done to the former by the latter—it isn't hard to understand the possibility of thinking, speaking and acting in terms of a liberating violence, of a redemptive violence.

If the élites of the Third World haven't the courage to rid themselves of their privileges and to bring justice to the millions living in sub-human conditions; if the governments concerned content themselves with reforms on paper, how can one restrain the youth who are tempted by radical solutions and violence? In the developed countries on both sides, how long will it be possible to restrain the ardour of youth, the spearhead of tomorrow's unrest, if the signs of disquiet and violence continue to multiply? How long will nuclear bombs be more powerful than the poverty bomb which is forming in the Third World?

Allow me the humble courage to take up a position on this issue. I respect those who feel obliged in conscience to opt for violence—not the all too easy violence of armchair guerilleros—but those who have proved their sincerity by the sacrifice of their life. In my opinion, the memory of Camilo Torres and of Che Guevara merits as much respect as that of Martin Luther King. I accuse the real authors of violence: all those who, whether on the right or the left, weaken justice and prevent peace. My personal vocation is that of a pilgrim of peace, following the example of Paul VI; personally, I would prefer a thousand times to be killed than to kill.

This personal position is based on the gospel. A whole life spent trying to understand and live the gospel has produced in me the profound conviction that if the gospel can, and should, be called revolutionary it is in the sense that it demands the conversion of each of us. We haven't the right to enclose ourselves within our egoism; we must open ourselves to the love of God and the love of men. But is it enough to turn to the beatitudes—the quintessence of the gospel message—to discover that the choice for christians seems clear: we christians are on the side of non-violence, which is by no means a choice of weakness or passivity. Non-violence means believing more passionately in the force of truth, justice and love than in the force of wars, murder and hatred.

If this appears to be mere moralising, be patient a moment. If the option for non-violence has its roots in the gospel, it is also based on reality. You ask me to be realistic? Here is my answer: If an explosion of violence should occur anywhere in the world, and especially in Latin America, you may be sure that the great powers would be immediately on the spot—even without a declaration of war—the super-powers would arrive and we would have another Vietnam. You ask for more realism? Precisely because we have to achieve a structural revolution it is essential to plan in advance a 'cultural revolution'—but in a new sense. For if mentalities do not undergo a radical change then structural reforms, reforms from the base, will remain at the theoretical stage, ineffective.

I should like now to address a few remarks especially to the young. To the youth of the under-developed countries I put this question: what is the point of acceding to power if you lack models adapted to your situation, to your countries? Up till now you have been offered solutions which are viable only for developed countries. While we christians try to exert a moral pressure, ever more courageously, on those who are responsible for the situation in our countries, you should try to prepare yourselves for the responsibilities that await you tomorrow; try above all to help the masses to become a people. You know only too well that material and physical underdevelopment leads to intellectual, moral and spiritual underdevelopment.

To the youth of developed countries, both capitalist and socialist, I would say: Instead of planning to go to the Third World to try and arouse violence there, stay at home in order to help your rich countries to discover that they too are in need of a cultural revolution which will produce a new hierarchy of values, a new world vision, a global strategy of development, the revolution of mankind.

Allow me to make one final remark. I have just come from Berlin, where I was invited to the World Congress of International Catholic Youth Movements. In that divided city I wondered how Europe could accept the dismembering of Berlin—symbol of so many divisions in the whole world. Why does mankind allow itself to be divided and torn asunder, from east to west, and even more profoundly from north to south?

It is only those who achieve an inner unity within themselves and possess a worldwide vision and universal spirit who will be fit instruments to perform the miracle of combining the violence of the prophets, the truth of Christ, the revolutionary spirit of the gospel— but without destroying love.

11
The church in the development of Latin America

An address prepared for the 10th Extraordinary Assembly of the Latin American Episcopal Council which took place at Mar del Plata (near Buenos Aires, Argentina) from 9 to 16 October 1966 on the theme: 'The active presence of the church in the development and integration of Latin America, in the light of the principles of the second Vatican Council.'

Preliminary remarks

(1) *Quality and extent of development*   Human alienation can result either from ignoring time in favour of eternity, or from ignoring eternity in favour of time. They are the two faces of alienation.

Marx would never have presented religion as the opium of the people and the church as alienated and alienator if he had seen around him a church made flesh, continuing the incarnation of Christ; if he had seen christians who really and practically loved men as the primary expression of their love for God; if he had seen the days of Vatican II, which sums up what theology can say about terrestrial reality.

It is clear that the transcendental side of man is as real as the economic. And moreover, we must remember an historic event of outstanding importance, now that man, who in twenty years has lived twenty thousand, is but a step from considering himself God: God himself was made man, to accomplish the divinisation of all men. Development therefore is the realisation of man in his full human dimension and, by the grace of God, in his divine dimension.

No country and no people can develop alone. The world has become inter-dependent. The presence of the church in the development of Latin America will be meaningful and effectual only in so far as it forms part of a total effort at presence in the world.

(2) *Social revolution and conversion* Who has no need of conversion, even conversions? We are all of us in need of continual conversion. And nations, which are an assembly of individuals, are all of them, without exception, in need of continual conversion. There are not innocent people and sinful people. The only difference lies in the concentration of faults, all of which arise—as in the case of individuals—from self-centredness.

The social revolution which the world needs will not come by act of parliament, nor by guerilla warfare, nor by war. It is a profound and radical transformation which presupposes divine grace, a movement of world opinion which can and must be helped and stimulated by the church of Latin America and of the whole world.

(3) *Responsibility of Latin American church* Latin-American society, since its discovery, has grown and

developed under the influence of the church. All its structures, social, economic, political and cultural, have undergone the influence of Iberian christianity. The struggles for independence brought about little change in these structures. Today, for the first time, we are witnessing the dawn of a substantial transformation. The church is indissolubly bound to this history, with its values, its authentic triumphs and moments of greatness, but also with its errors, its dissonances and aberrations.

Today, because of this, the church is faced with unquestionable responsibility and inescapable obligations. The church herself contributed to the authentic values of our civilisation and cannot permit them to be crushed by the strident advance of urgent and inevitable structural changes. But the church is also called to denounce collective sin, unjust and rigid structures, not simply as one who judges from without but as one who acknowledges her own share of the responsibility and of the blame. The church must be aware of her part in this history, and thus play her part with greater solidarity in the present and in the future.

Whatever the course of history, the fact is that the church today finds herself effectively present in a developing Latin America. This human situation of crisis in society demands a self-awakening on the part of the church, and a decisive effort to help the continent to achieve its liberation from underdevelopment. If this mission is to be fulfilled, the church must undergo a radical purification and conversion. Her relationships with the underdeveloped masses, with diverse groups and with all types of organisation, must become more and more relationships of service. Her strength must be calculated less in terms of prestige and power and more in terms of the gospel and of service to men. In this way, she will be in a position to reveal to the people of this anguished continent the true face of Christ.

(4) *Purpose of the church's presence*

(*a*) To help in the conversion of the continent. If Latin America desires the conversion of others, and especially of the developed world, it must sincerely and decisively begin by converting itself. It would have no moral force to speak to others if it lacked the courage to face up to its own defects as a people and to do everything possible to overcome them. Spiritual leaders, and the christian leaders in particular, have an important role in this conversion, above all because the impetus to reform must come from them.

(*b*) To stimulate in Latin America an awareness of its task in the world. No-one is in the world by chance. There is no such thing as chance, only divine providence. From all eternity, the humblest of men is present to the will of the Father and must fulfil his mission, whether it is great or small. What is important is that he should not opt out of the plan of love which regards men not as objects, but as subjects and co-creators.

If these remarks are valid for the individual, there is no reason why they should not hold for the nation. It was not by chance that Christopher Columbus landed in America. It was not by chance that our various peoples won their victories and suffered their defeats. And it is not by chance that we have our hopes and our disappointments. What is expected of us by the Father?

What must we do to conform to the plan of God? What is required of us that we be abreast of the times in which we are living?

This conference of the Latin American Episcopal Council, convened under the auspices of the Pontifical Commission for Latin America[1] to meditate on the presence of the church in the development of our continent, is a grace from God and we must do all in our power to correspond with this grace.

The shadow of sin over Latin America

(1) *Internal colonialism* It is probably not far wrong to say that the collective sin of Latin America, the synthesis of our sins as a people, is internal colonialism. This expression can give rise to equivocation and cause ill-feeling if it is not clearly explained. By 'internal colonialism', we mean the relationship of some developed regions with other underdeveloped regions in the same country (for example, the Brazilian industry of the South-Central has made large profits from the flow of raw materials supplied by the North-East and the North, both of which are still underdeveloped).

'Internal colonialism' means that a great part of rural Latin America continues to live in the middle ages. We need to find ways of expressing this which do not cause injury or, at least, which manifest love and concern in the manner of a surgeon who operates to save and to cure. Hiding the truth is not friendship. Nor is it friendship to proclaim the truth in a loveless manner. If one of the signs of our age is the ending of

[1] This commission was instituted by Pius XII in 1958, under the presidency of Cardinal Confalonieri, with Mgr Antonio Samoré from the Secretariat of State as vice-president.

colonialism (at least open political colonialism) how can we permit men to treat their fellow-countrymen in the way Europeans once treated Africans? We know that there are exceptions and are grateful for this. We have no wish to ignore the complexity of the situation and the circumstances which lead to blindness and to the apparent insensitivity which tolerates sub-human conditions of housing, clothing, food, education and work among the rural populations of our underdeveloped areas. And this is all the more understandable when, in addition, we consider:

(a) that some dioceses are often not in a position to treat the workers on their landed property in a less inhuman way;

(b) that this factor often creates an unconscious connivance between the property-owner and the diocese, which has no alternative but to use his chapel for religious ceremonies, for the patronal novena, for confirmation or for Sunday mass;

(c) that we would be extremely embarrassed if asked for an immediate solution, some way out of this situation.

(2) *The effect of defending privileges*
(a) Fear of a self-awakening. It is easy to say that Latin America is the catholic continent, the reserve of christianity for the whole world. But the Latin American masses will open their eyes, with us or without us or against us. There are no longer towering walls to separate peoples from one another. The means of

communication overcome any effort at isolation. And woe to christianity, when the eyes of the people are opened, if the masses have the impression that they were abandoned on account of the church's connivance with the rich and the powerful.

But apart from the risk of losing prestige in the eyes of the people—the problem is not one of prestige but of a mission to serve—it is our task, our human and christian duty to help the sons of God to emerge from the sub-human situation in which they now exist. Destitution degrades the human person and is an affront to the Creator and Father.

At this point we are advised to be prudent: it is easier and quicker (it is said) to open the eyes of the masses, to rouse them to consciousness, to make them aware of their situation, than it is to bring about structural reform. And if anyone, knowing this, promotes a self-awakening among the people—the pessimists say—he is playing with subversion, playing with communism, setting one class against the other.

It is striking to discover the extremes to which we are led by the defence of privileges. Concern with marxism would preserve religion as the opium of the people and the church as an alienating force. How can we ignore the beauty and the strength, the democracy and the christian potential of the endeavour to awaken the masses? It is a question of putting the creature on his feet, of arousing his sense of initiative, of working in groups, of a sense of responsibility; it is a question of altering the attitude which waits for the government to do everything.

Poverty which is transmitted from father to son, from grandfather to grandson, leaves marks which it is difficult to eradicate: the man who depends on others for everything, who is an outcast, an object of assistance and paternalism and not a subject of rights and justice; the man who is at the mercy of the good or ill will of an almighty boss (for whom there are no laws, no authority, no justice, and on whose judgment all depends) ends by acquiring the mentality of a slave. How can he avoid falling into fatalism and confusing dangerously the religion of his employer with the superstition and magic of the slaves? How can he avoid resigning himself to his fate, desperation, dejection today and rebellion tomorrow? The rudiments of education are not sufficient for cases like these, even if they are complemented by the fiction of voting rights.

We have no wish to ignore the complexity of the consequences of self-awakening, and we shall make some concrete suggestions in this regard. But for the present, let us admit a fear of such a self-awakening, which is in practice a conscious or unconscious defence of privileges.

(*b*) Distortion of christian principles. The christian principles invoked in defence of order are numerous— as if the concrete situation in our areas deserved the name of order. Absurd privileges are upheld in the name of the principle of property. Studies should be encouraged along the lines of the conclusions of the French Social Week which took place at Brest in June 1965, quoted by Don Manuel Larrain in his pastoral letter on development and bequeathed to his brothers in the episcopate as a most valuable witness: 'The revision of the notion of property, derived from liberal thinking and particularly from French legislation, concerns commercial property, which is one of the causes of the hardening of structures which militate against the recent requirements of development.'

The dignity of the human person is invoked as if the dignity of the workers were non-existent. Liberty is threatened and must be defended, but little is said about a liberty which has been crushed for centuries.

(c) *The communist bogey* The great expedient is the bogey of communism. And it is an easy bugbear to manipulate. Papal condemnations of atheistic communism are moved into position, together with the danger of the spread of communism throughout the world.

Anti-communism is as intolerant as communism itself. It admits of no choice other than its own. It contradicts itself by blatantly using, under the pretext of defending the human person, systems which offend human dignity, such as incitement to delation, prison on mere suspicion, fiscal or moral oppression. Without noticing it, it makes communist propaganda when it identifies communism with every courageous and intelligent act in defence of truth and justice.

The sins of the developed world

(1) *The flight from the essential* It is not easy to understand and accept something that runs contrary to our plans or upsets them excessively. But there comes a time when there is a danger of sinning against the light. When will the developed world grasp the mistaken nature of its relations with the underdeveloped countries?

It is by now commonplace to recall the event which

brought this fact home to us in a most striking way—the United Nations Assembly on commerce and development at Geneva in 1964. The Holy See had sent a team of representatives to the assembly, under the leadership of the late Fr Lebret. The fact is that if comparison is made between the investment in the underdeveloped world and the capital return, and, above all, between the loans made by the developed world and the losses suffered by the underdeveloped as a consequence of the prices imposed on their raw materials, the extortion cries to heaven for vengeance.

Let the developed world examine every proposal and make any sacrifice, provided it does not shirk the burning problem. Unfortunately, it is easier at times to give one's own blood than to deprive oneself of comfort and spend money. This is not said with resentment or irony, but is a simple recognition of the weakness of humanity, and not of any particular persons or countries.

(2) *Weak substitutes*

(*a*) Birth control. The relationship between underdevelopment and uncontrolled and irresponsible procreation is recognised by all underdeveloped countries. The developed countries, for their part, cling to this precious alibi: it is no good helping development without a previous drive to control the birth-rate, carried out on a national and even world level with technical proficiency and financial abandon.

It is essential to study deeply the problem of responsible parenthood. Certainly no foreign country has the right to impose the adoption of mass family planning as a condition of help given. This is a tremendous imposition, since it puts the irresistible pressure on poor populations of choosing between their hunger for food and culture and the reduction of their offspring.

When will the developed world take account of the spiritual problems involved in all this, of the trauma it creates, of the violence it commits? The question is too delicate to be resolved from without. We must decisively and courageously vindicate the responsibility of the magisterium to judge responsible parenthood and to give precise directions. Seeing that the interdependence between demographic factors and economic development is still a controversial point even among specialists, no approval can be given to the experiments which are being carried out even in our own continent to control the growth of population, without taking into consideration the ethical and cultural characteristics and the spiritual point of view of the people concerned. The primary need is rather to bring about a profound, rapid and global transformation of the socio-economic structures, to prepare a fitting place in human society for the new generations.

(b) For and against volunteers. When a developed country offers more than money and tries to send people—its own children, its youth, its technicians—it is difficult not to accept, delicate to refuse. At best, one can give the impression of being ungrateful and bad-mannered. It could be considered a greed for money on the part of a country which lacks the technical capacity, perhaps even the honesty, to put it to the best use.

And so we get the volunteers. There is no question of suspicion being levelled at them as if they were dangerous infiltrators or fifth columnists. Anyone who has contact with them, and particularly with the young, may feel that they lack experience and adaptability, but credit must be given for their generosity and capacity for sacrifice. And their exposure to sub-human reality brings about a profound change in them which creates problems on their return home. But here again, it must be said with all respect, we are not reaching the nub of the problem.

(c) Excessive food production. This is another delicate question, another alibi clothed in generosity and presenting positive aspects. We can understand a benefactor's need to render accounts and to make propaganda, but some progress will have to be made in the shameful and often humiliating manner of giving aid. And clearly, offers of food, which represents the surplus food production of the donors, should not enter into commercial competition with the food products of the receiving country.

Starvation is on the increase in the underdeveloped world, and we cannot permit ourselves the luxury of reducing the quantity of food which comes into our country. But our bonds of friendship and brotherhood are close enough to enable us to point out, with the greatest delicacy, that donations alone cannot clear the conscience of the donor, because there remains always the problem of justice.

In this respect, a good example is being given by the European and North American churches, who are working generously for international cooperation and developing its aims and methods. This could have positive repercussions on the general problem of relations between developed and underdeveloped worlds. The ideal is to discover the most equitable way of development, in close collaboration with the national bodies of the countries concerned: the planning and the criteria of priority in the application of available means must be elaborated by interested national groups who are in close contact with the reality. In this way, we shall avoid even the appearance of a veiled colonialism or an intolerable international paternalism, and open out prospects of international justice.

Concrete proposals

(1) *United action against internal colonialism* The Latin-American Episcopal Council (CELAM) must stimulate the national social organisations of the various episcopal conferences of the continent:

(*a*) to draw up a solid body of evidence designed to demonstrate the urgency of defeating internal colonialism;

(*b*) to give strong, charitable and constructive guidance to those who colonise in their own territory, but who are desirous of taking their place in the peaceful social revolution and lack the knowledge or the courage for the final decision;

(*c*) to convince the bishops of the continent that to leave a small group of the people of God to shoulder the burden of denouncing the grave abuses of the system—and if we do not denounce them we shall not be forgiven by those who benefit today but tomorrow will be the victims—is to abandon them to the injustice of being accused of subversion and communism.

(2) *United action to awaken the masses* CELAM must stimulate the various episcopal conferences of the continent to examine:

124

(*a*) the quickest, most efficient and most constructive method of bringing about a self-awakening in the Latin-American masses, so as not to sin by omission on the one hand, and on the other to avoid armed conflict or the hatred which leads to blood;

(*b*) the possibility and suitability of organising non-violent action without delay on a continental scale, in favour of the human development of the Latin-American masses at present living in sub-human conditions.

(3) *Reform of christian social principles*   CELAM must stimulate the episcopal conferences of the continent to examine again the christian social principles which are in danger of being warped, such as the principle of property. Some rapid and sure means must be found to publish widely the results of such study and to give directives for a common effort.

(4) *Attitude to anti-communism*   CELAM must stimulate the episcopal conferences to make a special point of avoiding the use and abuse of the anti-communist bogey. The people of God must be put on their guard against the errors of communism (and the fact that, according to the Holy See, socialism is not necessarily identified with the denial of God, is a great step forward) just as they must be on their guard against the materialist roots of capitalism. But the people of God must also take care not to set up obstacles, in the name of anti-communism, to human advancement and to the defence of rights essential to the dignity of sons of God.

(5) *Latin America's number one problem*   CELAM must stimulate the episcopal conferences to review the con-

tinent's 'number one problem', as it is called, and this, contrary to what we have thought and said, is not vocations to the priesthood, but underdevelopment. We must not insult God by attributing the shortage of vocations to the objective and systematic refusal by his sons in Latin America to follow the light. We must not regard as the cause what is in fact the consequence. Let us have courage and revise the whole question of vocations.

The man in a sub-human situation is not in any condition—unless a miracle occurs—to train for the priesthood, since understanding and willing become a reality only at a certain level of human life. Willing is a luxury for one who vegetates: he doesn't will anything, to be a priest, to be anything.

(6) *Concern for youth* This is the age of youth throughout the whole world. The phenomenon in Latin America takes on a serious character, since half the population is under twenty years of age. Young people today, particularly in the universities, have not only the right but the duty to interest themselves in national and international problems. And it is sad to observe the great flight from school of our young people in many areas of the continent: of those who begin elementary school in the North-East, only 1 % reach the university.

Let CELAM stimulate the episcopal conferences of the continent to work with bishops, priests and, above all, parents and teachers, towards an understanding of today's youth and a real effort at formation.

(7) *The importance of land reform* While we must acknowledge the efforts of certain countries, the land problem is still serious and becoming more complex.

The 'land reform' laws, promulgated ten years ago (similar legislation exists in almost all the countries of Latin America) do not unfortunately solve the problems of the land workers, especially of the great mass of farm-hands and small plot-owners. Discontent and revolt are manifested everywhere. Agricultural production and zootechnics have not kept pace with the increasing population; technological progress has been slight in the sphere of agriculture; the technique of planning and administration of rural activity is still in the initial stages; financial means are insufficient; there is a serious shortage of specialised technicians. Government institutions for assisting farmers are not adequate for the needs.

The most serious problem, in this context, is the property structure, which can be characterised as follows:

(a) the preservation of land monopoly, with the expansion and immobilisation of non-productive land;

(b) the frightening growth of anti-economic mining property;

(c) the persistence of feudalism in labour relations particularly in areas where agriculture is not diversified (sugar cane, coffee, bananas, cattle).

As a consequence of this we must note:

(a) an increase in food imports;

(b) malnutrition of great masses of the people;

(c) sub-human living conditions of the peasants, without possibility of education, of a higher standard of health or living, of purchasing power.

The result is that the Latin-American land problem,

because of its importance in the life of the whole continent (particularly in the economic sphere because we live on primary products which must occupy the greater part of the population in rural activity), must be seen as a problem which interests, concerns and threatens the whole society.

Let CELAM therefore examine and discuss the more recent studies of the land situation in Latin America, and make its proposals. Let it support, by means of a campaign to inform public opinion, the movement for authentic land reform, large-scale reform and not pilot projects or ineffectual colonising. Let it take into account the land question in all its activity in support of development programmes and capital investment. With respect for the democratic order, let it give special attention to the movements for the organisation of the peasants and small plot-owners. Let it be on guard, as never before, against the counter-reform movements in various countries, and against false land reforms which will promote neither the redistribution of property nor the national wealth.

Christian presence in the Third World

(1) *Economic bolivarism* A study of the work of Simon Bolívar shows us that political independence is nominal unless it is completed by economic independence. More than a century has passed since Bolívar, and the Latin-American countries, all politically independent, are still fighting desperately for economic independence. 'Economic bolivarism' means support for the Latin-American Common Market. An alliance between the excessively strong and the excessively weak is impossible.

128

The European Common Market demands the over-coming of regional meanness in favour of the greater common good. Without the moral support of the Latin-American hierarchy and the collaboration of all the people of God, our countries will not overcome their natural vanity and they will not acknowledge their mutual interdependence which is the prerequisite for the realisation of the Latin-American Common Market and for an effective dialogue between Latin America and Europe, and between Latin America and North America.

CELAM, after more than ten years of growth and efficiency, can and must serve as the inspiration and model for the development of the continent.

(2) *Support for understanding the Third World* There is not the slightest wish to isolate the underdeveloped countries and to inspire in them a hatred for the affluent. We are dealing here rather with our need to overcome selfishness. Africa has much to offer us and much to gain from our political experience and our support; with the collaboration of the whole world, there will be a new dimension and a solution to the problems of Asia.

The purpose of the Latin-American Common Market is not to close the continent in on itself, nor to oppose anyone, least of all its closest brothers, the underdeveloped countries. The Latin-American Episcopal Conference, under the auspices of CELAM, can and must initiate contacts with the African and Asiatic episcopal conferences, with a view to spiritual relationships which will create a bond of solidarity between the three continents.

(3) *Public opinion and justice* The progress of the underdeveloped world clearly presupposes the vigorous participation of the underdeveloped peoples themselves. But there are some decisions of an international scale which require international collaboration.

It is admitted by all that peace without equality is utopia. It can be fully demonstrated, moreover, that the relations between the developed and underdeveloped worlds are basically a problem of justice on a world scale. We need a strong movement of public opinion with sufficient moral force to shake the world, to shake all men of all countries, developed and underdeveloped, the universities, the press and radio, the religious and intellectual leaders, the politicians, employers and workers.

CELAM should ask the pope, the pilgrim of peace, to call an extraordinary assembly of representatives from the hierarchy of the whole world, developed and underdeveloped, with the specific objective of examining the possibility of such a movement by the whole people of God. Only in this way shall we succeed in making everyone understand that the relations between rich and poor countries constitute a problem of the greatest urgency, which must be studied by the light of justice for the attainment of true peace in the world.

I have not wished, in this address, to put aside or ignore the subjects planned for the Mar del Plata conference, themes which are indispensable for an efficacious presence of the church in the development of Latin America. It would be unjust to forget or undervalue the magnificent work for Latin America done up to now by CELAM and by CAL. For this reason I have concentrated on some practical aspects of the problems, which require study and decision.

12
Development
without justice

This document was published by the Catholic Workers'
Action (ACO) of north-east Brazil on 1 May 1967. It is
an inquiry into the social situation of the North-East,
conducted by the ACO and published in Recife under
the patronage of its archbishop, Dom Helder Camara,
who was its inspiration.

This document is born of the anguish and sense of
responsibility of a group of workers in the North-East,
engaged in the Catholic Workers' Action, after an
analysis of the situation of the working classes of the
region said to be 'in full development'.

It is not directed to any person or group in particular, but to all who have a share of the responsibility,
who have 'eyes to see and ears to hear' and a heart to
love. It is directed to every man of goodwill, rich or
poor, ruler or subject, employer or worker, employed
or unemployed, christian or non-christian, believer or
atheist. It is directed, in particular, to the North-East,
and to those of the North-East who are involved in the
situation of misery and underdevelopment.

The document does not present detailed, concrete solutions, because the mission of the ACO is essentially evangelical. The object is first of all to stir the conscience by means of truth, because without truth authentic dialogue is impossible. In presenting the truth, it is our intention to challenge all men to a courageous dialogue which will lead to concrete solutions.

Although the cases quoted are isolated, they indicate a general situation of lack of respect for man, and they have been chosen almost at random from a large volume of facts gathered throughout the whole of the North-East, from Maranhao to Bahia. Anything which could identify persons or undertakings is generally avoided, because the purpose is only to draw out the significance of the attitudes.

They are attitudes which cry out for modification. It is our hope that this document may help the reader to discover new values and to acquire a permanent attitude of concern for justice and respect for the dignity of man. We have all cooperated in this work and are responsible for it.

I. The worker in the developing North-East

The Brazilian North-East is currently the centre of the attention of the American continent, not only on account of the concentration and gravity of the socio-economic problems, but principally because it is here more than anywhere else in Latin America that planned development is being experienced at its most consistent and rational. While retaining the characteristics of an underdeveloped region, the North-East has expanded economically more than any other area of Brazil, due principally to heavy investment in electric power, roads, irrigation etc., and to an aggressive policy of industrialisation, encouraged by a combination of fiscal incentives and capital aid.

One of the characteristics of the North-East is the abundance of available labour, residing in huts in the great human agglomerations of the larger cities and forming quarters which have risen spontaneously and increase day by day in proportion to the flow of migrants from the inland to the coast. These quarters are to be found all over Latin America, and are given various names—*alagados* in Recife, *favelas* in Rio de Janeiro and S Paulo, *malocas* in Rio Grande, *alagados* or *invazao* in Bahia, *vila miséria* in Argentina, *invasión* or *tugurios* in Colombia, *barriada* in Peru, *quilombo* in Panama. They are concentrated in great contingents of unemployed in the North-East. They are men and women with large families, mostly unskilled, who are badly-paid, under-paid, or simply unemployed.

In Recife, the capital of Pernambuco, the phenomenon is more manifest than in other places, and it has more serious consequences on account of the fact that Recife is the pole of major attraction for immigrants because of its greater social progress, both economic and cultural. More than 30% of the total population of the state of Pernambuco is concentrated in the so-called 'greater Recife', which comprises the capital and four zones on the periphery, and represents only 1·5% of state territory.

What is called 'available and cheap labour' is nothing other, therefore, than an immense legion of under-employed or unemployed, without qualification or opportunity for work. In 1965, we were informed by SUDENE that there were more than one million unemployed in the great urban zones of the North-East.

These details and figures show, in some way, the reduction of the worker of the North-East to marginal status in the development drive which is going on in our region. The technicians examine the index of global expansion, they pursue economic goals, they are concerned with estimates and incidence of investments and then they display the graphs which mathematically reflect the rhythm of our region's enrichment. But perhaps they do not notice the criminal contradiction which they are helping to construct: in the measure in which the wealth of the region increases with development, the number of 'marginals' increases also, of those who do not participate in this wealth, who do not benefit from this development. The analysis of the reality and the plans are elaborated in inaccessible offices, by men who, by reason of their professional formation, approach the most painful phenomena with the cold objectivity of technology. What do they know of the worker? Have they any concern to harmonise development techniques with the demands of social justice?

On the other hand, what does the worker know of the industrial development plans of the region? Who has ever explained to him the significance of modernising production processes? He understands nothing of the importance of specialist labour in development. He scarcely knows anything about development.

In raising these problems, the ACO does not take up a position against development. In the 'Manifesto on the Situation of the Workers in the North-East' (March

1966), the ACO affirmed that 'only development can create the structural conditions which will make possible the welfare of all'. But as the manifesto also stated, 'the various stages of development must consider man in relation to himself and to the society in which he lives, not only because man is the primary goal of development, but also because he must be its principal agent by his conscious participation in the economico-social changes.'

From a human and social point of view, what is happening in the North-East is a distortion of the true object of development, which is the advancement of 'man and all of men', to quote François Perroux, one of the most quoted theorists in the whole country, including the North-East.

The effects of development fall most frequently on the worker of the North-East, affecting his life and his mentality by the suffering and hopelessness which arise as a consequence of the distortions which progress is generating in our region.

Development is a cycle of conflicts. Conflicts between governments and undertakings, between progressive and conservative undertakings, between old interests and new, internal and external structures, etc. And the worker is a victim of these conflicts, because he has no defence, he has no preparation for defending himself. Thus, while it is affirmed that 'the North-East is the most expanding region of Brazil', the working class of the North-East suffers an expanding misery which can be described as follows:

(a) lower wages which are contrary to law;

(b) a progressive increase of unemployment and under-employment brought about by industrial modernisation;

(c) a general climate of exploiting the worker;

(d) a growth in incidence and cunning in the violation of labour laws;

(e) the absence of any policy of creating more jobs, resulting in a progressive widening of the gap between the supply of new jobs (very small) and the supply of labour (very great).

We are witnessing, in the North-East, the substitution of a feudal structure by a capitalist structure, and as active christians we cannot do other than manifest a profound fear at the materialist way in which capitalism tackles its problems, without concern for man, who can be used simply as a figure in the planning statistics.

This fear grows from day to day as we see the symptoms of an economy characterised by the employment of capital to greatest advantage and by the liberal pragmatism which makes profit the primary goal. Large private groups, natives and foreigners, are set up in the region to take over the direction of the regional economy; the dominant economic concepts in the industrialisation process are almost exclusively based on the laws of supply and demand; the determining factor in the great sectoral reforms (sugar cane, textile industries, etc) is the fluctuation in the markets dominated by national and international capitalism.

SUDENE, which bears the responsibility for regional planning, uses as the principal instrument of development a combination of stimuli to industrialisation, which only concern the interests of capital and are specially suited to large financial undertakings, in other words to the great economic groups. As a consequence, there is a tendency which could become irreversible towards a concentration of wealth in the hands of those who are already wealthy.

Meanwhile the worker of the North-East continues to be treated as 'available cheap labour', without any possibility of negotiating his labour hire in a highly technological industrialisation, because:

(a) The work factor has a limited place in the production process which is being set up, in which the machine substitutes for the man with greater efficiency.

(b) The jobs which are created demand, in most cases, a specialist qualification which the worker of the North-East does not possess, for lack of opportunity.

In view of the inevitability of this type of industrialisation, which does not solve the unemployment problem and therefore does not create the possibility of a just distribution of wealth, it would be legitimate to hope that SUDENE already had policies and means for correcting tendencies in regional development, which leave man at the margin of the process.

But this is not the case. In agriculture, for example, which occupies 70% of the population of the North-East, there is a situation of misery and hunger and injustice and, what is more serious, no prospect of immediate improvement. The development programmes for zootechnics are too timid or simply deceptive. And the reason for this seems to be a lack of courage in making radical reforms which will change the archaic structure so that production may increase and the rural worker may have access to the land. What is being done is almost exclusively to the benefit of the great landowners for whom the financing systems function. The small farmer, without credit, without technical assistance, without the means of trade expansion, usually loses his profit to the middleman and to the speculator and often enough falls into the cycle of misery.

In consequence the great mass of rural people, our brothers in the country areas, suffer all sorts of injustice, the greatest and commonest of which is the lack of regular work, and this leads them to accept every type of exploitation practised by the employers, or to emigrate to the urban centres in search of opportunities denied to them by agriculture. It is this emigrant mass which expands the borders of the slums and forms the 'available cheap labour' which acts as a bait for southern and foreign businessmen.

The lot of the city workers is no different from that of the land workers, because unemployment, injustice and exploitation unite them in the same drama and because both are victims of the same errors, the same omissions, the same distortion of economic planning. They are immersed in illiteracy, in humiliating housing conditions, in begging, in endemic diseases, in infant mortality, in violated dignity, in malnutrition; they have no schools for their children, there is no life in their trade unions, they are unemployed, they have no social welfare, and they lack leadership. In brief, they are to be found in the margin of progress. Their hope too lies in integral solutions which will give to economic development the social dimension which is demanded by human dignity.

As christians studying the problems of the working class of the developing North-East, the members of the

ACO keep in mind the teaching of Pope John XXIII in *Mater et Magistra*:

Social progress must accompany and be joined to economic development in such a way that all social categories may benefit from the increase in the national income. Care must be taken therefore, and serious efforts must be made to see, that there is no increase in the economic and social imbalance, but rather that it should diminish as far as possible.

It follows from this that the economic wealth of a people does not result only from the global abundance of goods, but still more from its just and effective distribution, which must ensure the full personal development of the community members, because this and this alone is the goal of the national economy.

The members of ACO, studying and gathering together in this document the contemporary problems of the working class in the North-East, especially as regards the lack of respect for human dignity, do so with the sense of responsibility which derives from complete acceptance of the further teaching of *Mater et Magistra*: 'Let every citizen feel responsible for the realisation of the common good, in all the sectors of national life'. But they accept it principally in order to fulfil their proper mission, which is to evangelise. Evangelisation must be tied to life, because only in that way is it possible to reach the whole man, body and soul. Our example is Christ, who always joined to the work of evangelisation an attention and concern for men, healing the sick, multiplying the loaves, changing water into wine.

II. Need for vigilance

The need for vigilance, which is imposed on the members of the ACO and on all conscientious citizens who feel responsible for the world in which they live, arises, in the case of the North-East, not only from the teaching of the church and of the scriptures, but mainly from the comparison of those teachings with the reality of the worker's life.

Dom Helder Camara, archbishop of Olinda and Recife, who has spoken over a number of years in the North-East and in various countries of the world on the necessity of founding on justice the relationships between employer and worker, superior and subject, rich nations and poor, in 1966 gave a series of conferences to graduates, awakening them to the reality and to the necessity of watchfulness. On 16 December in the same year, he told finalists in the school of chemistry at the Federal University of Pernambuco:

> Think of the joy of the head of the family when he gets work; the anxiety of the unemployed; the sorrow of those who are sacked; the children who do the work of adults ... you will discover that if life begins at forty for others, it ends at thirty-five for the workers. You will discover how, almost always, the price of remaining in the factory and taking advantage of what it offers is to forgo using the intelligence or indulging in ideas, to put aside the possibility of willing and choosing.

Five days later, speaking to his own students in the Catholic University of Pernambuco, he said:

> We have the right and the duty to sound all the warnings we think necessary; to denounce whenever

it is necessary; to stimulate, to question, to suggest, to discourage, to encourage, to call upon men and to speak about God. The basis of our right consists in the fact that the fate of the people is at stake, and they are our people, flesh of our flesh, blood of our blood.

We cannot remain silent, therefore, when, as happened recently in S Luiz (Maranhao) at a meeting of workers in a slum area, twelve men trying to solve the problem of water supply reached the conclusion that this basic convenience was denied them, because the 80,000 cruzeiros (approx £10[1]) to pay for connecting the water from the mains to the houses was not available. These twelve men were all heads of families, and only four of them had steady work.

We cannot remain silent when we know that even the so-called RITA project, started in the North-East by Prof Morris Azimow and designed to activate the community from within by setting up small and medium-sized industries using local raw materials, is betraying its aims in the extent to which the adoption of advanced technology has reduced the power of labour absorption, while the treatment given to workers in the existing factories differs in no way from the general treatment. In Cariri Cearense, where the RITA project is in full swing, the workers are labouring under humiliating conditions. In a ceramic factory, for example, the work is exhausting and dangerous to health. Apart from the fact that very few get their cards signed and receive a family wage, no-one is paid sickness benefit, not even the men who work in the

[1] £1.00=7,680 Old Cruzeiros (June 1968). A New Cruzeiro was introduced in 1966 and the current rate (January 1969) is £1.00=9.05 Cr.

furnaces where the raw materials are burned and where the heat is so excessive that a man cannot normally work there for more than a year. In another factory in the same place, shameful wages are paid. In the box-making department, one of the best-paid women receives scarcely 4,600 cruzeiros a week. Nonetheless, the RITA project is held up and praised as one of the great instruments of regional development.

We cannot remain silent when we witness the multiplication of the great concentrations of human leftovers in the major cities, particularly in the capital of the state, and when we see no public effort to face the causes and consequences of this problem. Wretched slums have grown up in all the capitals, where thousands of families, wrapped in rags, seek refuge. And these quarters proliferate and enlarge in the midst of filth and waste, as happens at S Luiz.

We cannot remain silent when thousands of workers in the whole of the North-East are forced out of work by the modernisation of their factories. This redundancy is as high as 50% of the workers in some cases, for example a textile factory in Fortaleza.

We cannot look on with indifference when we know that the great majority of undertakings in the North-East utilise the excess labour supply to pay any wages they like to the workers, frequently even breaking the minimum wage law. The Recife worker who, after six months of unemployment, was forced to accept the 12,000 cruzeiros offered to him by a cloth factory, is not an isolated case.

These examples, quoted at random from among hundreds gathered by the ACO throughout the entire North-East, constitute, individually or jointly, a denunciation of the rejection of the working class in the development of the North-East. This rejection is characterised, among other ways, by the ignorance which leaves the workers to their own development; by the contradiction between the increase in the gross income of the region and the growing poverty of the great mass of workers; by the isolation in which the workers are left on the questions which directly concern them and affect their lives, as in the reform of the textile industry, of the industrialisation policy, and of labour training schemes, in which agreements are reached solely between the technicians and the employers, between the government and the business concern; by the conviction of the technicians that they cannot delay over questions of social justice, because that would retard economic development.

Has God really created two types of humanity: one who asserts himself and gets rich and the other who just suffers and withers? Can it be that all men have not got the same ultimate goal, the same human and divine vocation to be fulfilled?

III. Paternalism in the rejection of the worker

The lack of an official policy on the integration, in a conscious way, of the working class in the process of development, encourages the attitude of contempt for the rights and dignity of the workers. The paternalist solutions which act as a cover for injustice, function as a process which removes the worker still more to the margin of development. Paternalism seeks the surrender of conscience, the blunting of opposition, the compromise of the worker with interests opposed to his class. In a word, silence is bought at the price of crushing human dignity.

Paternalism assumes various forms and uses various techniques to reach the same object. It is indicated in the isolated attitudes of every employer and of every undertaking, but it reflects a collective state of mind in which official or semi-official welfare schemes can be identified.

In the more morally repugnant cases, paternalism is simply a cover for exploiting the very destitution of the workers. In Pernambuco, for example, the owner of a factory, who didn't pay even the minimum regional wage, presented himself as candidate in the local elections and got the votes of most of his workers in return for sums ranging from three to five thousand cruzeiros.

The cases differ in details but they have the same characteristics. A Cearense factory had decided to commemorate Christmas with a kind message of human solidarity, of christian fraternity, of peace on earth and glory to God on high. But at the end of the week they deducted one day's wages for Christmas Day. And another factory helped the workers to buy bicycles, sewing machines, etc, and deducted the payments each week. This is the price of silence, because when someone complains or shows that he is not satisfied, however legitimate his reason may be, he is simply punished with immediate dismissal.

In general, the workers are closed in an attitude of compromise and acceptance, also because the example of the suffering and persecution of their colleagues who had the courage to react discourages them from any worthier attitude. But the compromise of workers can be explained also by a combination of negative circumstances: fear and insecurity, hunger and necessity, lack of awareness and lack of formation, the social weakness of the class, due to the absence of enlightened leaders and general lack of confidence in themselves as individuals.

Fear and insecurity, the permanent risk of unemployment and the arbitrary rule of the law of might confirm the worker in his attitude of resignation to his lot. The situation is aggravated because the lack of leaders and representatives deepens in them a psychosis of fear, so weak do they feel and abandoned.

They are afraid also of being considered 'subversive', the usual term for anyone who yields to the temptation to complain. And fear sinks into the life and mentality of the worker: the fear of speaking, the fear of listening, even the fear of thinking.

And the fear of starvation. The case of the worker, who fainted three times in a factory in Escada (Pernambuco) is not uncommon, nor infrequent. Cases of pupils who faint in the classroom occur all over the North-East. The malnutrition of almost the entire working population of the North-East is confirmed and denounced by all the researches done in the region, one of which, very recently, under the responsibility of the Joaquim Nabuco Institute of Social Research, revealed, among other frightening facts, that only 20% of the population of Mata succeed in getting eggs to eat.

The reality is faced by the public authorities with long-term solutions together with economic doctrine as orthodox as it is self-sufficient, as if economics were the absolute science and the highest value for humanity. Meanwhile, grand assistance programmes are started to gloss over the facts, and they have the merit of satisfying hunger for a few days of the month, but they destroy men with humiliation. Such is the case with the 'Food for Peace' programme and the 'Alliance for Progress', and of other similar official alms-giving, which regionalise the spirit of begging and destroy the capacity to fight for human advancement.

Birth control gains ground as a solution in such a situation, and today is practised in the North-East (Bahia, Pernambuco and Ceara) at the level of scientific research, in which the women workers become guinea-pigs, persuaded by the evidence of their own poverty which will not support a large family. Instead of education and the creation of more jobs and repression of labour exploiting, the solution is the mechanical sterilisation of women.

All these processes have an alienating effect on the worker, rendering him less active in the development of which he should be the 'principal agent and beneficiary'. In this respect, it is worth giving an extract from a letter sent by the superior general of the Jesuits in December 1966 to the superiors of his congregation in Latin America: 'We must not think, moreoever, that the powerful classes should be the principal agents of a radical and more just structural transformation. The reform of society, according to equitable and human canons of justice, concerns above all the poor, the worker, all those social classes who are now forced to live on the margin of society, without a just share of its goods and services and without participating in its decisions...'

If we reflect more deeply on the situation of the working class in the North-East, we shall discover a deplorable and general incapacity on the part of the worker to discover the greatness of his human dignity. The victims of deformed systems inherited from the past, of distortions in modern processes and structures, and of the selfishness of the privileged minority who benefit from the present situation, the workers have not even the advantage of an influx of ideas and currents of opinion which might open their eyes and make possible for them an effective participation in life, in society and in the world. Ignorance and illiteracy are an obstacle to ambition and force them to resign themselves to the style of life imposed on them by society. This is perhaps why they are regarded and treated by many theorists not as constructive elements in development, but as useless and dead weight, which gives rise to an attitude of paternalism and pushes the worker still further on to the margin.

The necessity of an education policy geared to the advancement of the working class is recognised in a document written by a group of experts in education and community activity, published by SUDENE and presented at the seminar on education and development, which was held in December 1966 at Recife. The following passages are taken from this paper:

A fundamental problem will be the utilisation and development of the human means, that is the intelligence, the attitudes and the capacity of each person in the community. Thus it will be necessary that every man, as an agent of development, shall be able to acquire a professional qualification, to create new habits, new capacities, new values and aspirations which will permit him an effective participation in the expansion process, whether of receiving its goods

147

and services or of supplying them. The chief means of promoting such a development is given to us by education.

On the other hand, considering man as the beneficiary of development, accessible conditions must be created which will enable him to integrate himself into the world and its human institutions, to enjoy the cultural benefits of learning, art, literature, to develop his activities and widen his interests, to use his leisure time and develop affective and social relationships of mutual enrichment.

Development which has access to the greatest possible quantity of material goods as its sole aim, runs the risk of turning man against himself, by reducing him to the category of consumer and competitor.

A policy of this nature must be applied to all the working class and, in particular, to the young workers, who move from one job to the other, without the opportunity for specialisation, a constant source of worry for the Young Catholic Workers (JOC).

IV. General situation of injustice

John XXIII, in his encyclical *Pacem in Terris*, gave to the world norms of community life and of social and political organisation, in the light of which it is a duty to point out every situation of injustice and disorder suffered by the working class in the North-East. We quote:

In a well-constituted and efficient community life, it is a fundamental principle that every human being is a person: that is, a nature bestowed with intelligence and free will. For this reason, he possesses in himself rights and duties emanating directly and simultaneously from his own nature. It is a question therefore of rights and duties which are universal, inviolable and inalienable. And if we consider the dignity of the human person by the light of revealed truths, our esteem is incomparably greater.

In treating of the rights of man, we must first take note that the human being has the right of existence, the right to physical integrity, to a fitting standard of living: this means, in particular, food, clothing, housing, relaxation, health benefit, the indispensable social services. It follows from this that the person has also the right to be protected in the case of illness, of infirmity, of widowhood, in old age, in enforced unemployment, and in every other privation of the means of sustenance due to circumstances outside his control.

There derives also from human nature the right of participation in cultural goods and, therefore, the right to basic education and to a technical and professional formation consonant with the level of cultural development of the respective community.

As regards economic activity, it is clear that, from natural necessity, the person is entitled not only to freedom of initiative, but also to work.

In the Brazilian North-East, where the teachings of Pope John XXIII have been and are still praised and quoted, men who defend and proclaim the 'christian and democratic way of life' stoop to the most shameful humiliations of the human dignity of the workers, as happened in the case of a worker in Paulista (Pernambuco) who, having lost his fingers at work, was dismissed with the remark from his employer that he could return when his fingers had grown. Or as happened in the cloth factory at Fortaleza (one of many in the North-East which adopt the same system), where all workers, on taking up employment, are forced to sign a document which renounces their right to signed labour cards, social assistance and membership of trade unions.

There is not only a breach of the fundamental laws of social ethics in all the cases quoted, but a scandalous evasion even of Brazilian legislation. And it is always the humble and defenceless whose rights and dignity are trampled on.

Injustice in the relations between capital and work is so open and immune as to acquire the force of custom, almost of law. It spreads in the measure in which examples of impunity convince the more timid employers they can use the same methods in exploiting labour, using pressure-tactics and persecution, wage swindles and destruction of the stability achieved.

Examples of labour exploitation:

(a) Granting only four hours rest to a worker suffering from hepatitis, when the doctor ordered him 30 days (Fortaleza).

(b) Keeping workers of more than four years in the same firm without records, without full payment for hours worked, without holidays and without access to the benefits of social assistance (Recife).

(c) Not paying for the overtime worked to satisfy demand for the product manufactured (Natal).

(d) Not paying the wage increases guaranteed by contract and by collective agreement, constraining the

150

workers and their families to a situation of hunger while the cost of living continues to rise (S Luiz).

(*e*) Removing elderly workers and replacing them with younger who are paid less (Alagoas, textile factory).

(*f*) Not granting to domestics their right to holidays, to weekly time off, to fixed hours, in brief to human treatment.

The pressure on the workers, aided by a climate of persecution which aims at destroying all capacity for resistance and reaction on the part of the workers, takes the following forms:

(*a*) Specialised workers and even section heads and supervisors are transferred to manual work such as cleaning (S Luiz, Fortaleza, Recife, Paulista, Aracaju, especially in the textile industry).

(*b*) Brazilians ignored for appointments as supervisor in favour of foreigners, who are better paid and in league with the employers, and assume arrogant and violent attitudes towards their Brazilian subordinates, although most of them needed the help of the Brazilians in order to familiarise themselves with production techniques (Fortaleza).

(*c*) Workers with many years service and even supervisor status, are offended and humiliated by expressions and attitudes designed to render them incapable of their work, so that they will accept unjust agreements. In one of these cases, in Pernambuco, a worker with more than thirty years' service, after an episode like this was so confused and revolted that he collapsed later at home and died.

(*d*) Workers suffer partial infirmity (blindness, for example) after many years of service in the same concern, and they are pushed about from one man to the other, from one duty to the other (Aracaju, textile factory).

Swindles and injustices over wages are so well known that they need no examples. It is notorious and public knowledge that in commerce thousands of clerks, from Maranhao to Bahia in the North-East, are obliged to sign receipts for minimum wages when in fact they are paid less. In one of the most important textile factories in Recife (800 workers), the majority of the workers have more than ten years service and are paid less than the regional minimum. And also at Recife, several public transport companies pay their ticket collectors less than half the minimum wage, but require a receipt for the full amount.

The worst victims of these injustices are the workers with more than ten years' service. The fight against the stability of the workers has been transformed in the employers' campaign throughout the North-East. There are cases of every type which show that the methods have reached perfection, without consideration for rights acquired, or legal guarantees, or the consequences for the families of the stable workers who have been dismissed :

(*a*) In Aracaju a worker with 26 years of service was forced to accept dismissal for only 100,000 cruzeiros (approx £15).

(*b*) In one factory in Natal no worker is permitted more than five years of continuous work. When he reaches the third or fourth year, he is summarily dismissed and another is put in his place.

(c) At Fortaleza, and in almost the whole of the region, there are factories which systematically dismiss their workers before the end of their first year, so that they can re-accept them afterwards for a new period.

(d) In a factory at Paulista the office assistants were, for the most part, elderly workers without specialised skill but with many years of experience. Recently, those with more than twenty years of service were obliged to pass on their knowledge and experience to young people just taken on, who already earned higher wages and soon replaced their elders. And because the older workers refused the conditions of dismissal which the firm proposed, they were despatched without scruple to another department, and shortly afterwards simply dismissed.

At Paulista also, a stable worker, who yielded to pressure and accepted his dismissal for 800,000 cruzeiros, twice attempted suicide because of the destitution in which he lives with his family.

In March 1966, the ACO, in a manifesto (already quoted), made public knowledge the situation of the workers in the North-East, especially as regards the crimes against employment stability. From then on the situation deteriorated still more, notwithstanding the repercussions produced by the manifesto, which even aroused some civil and military authorities.

V. Textile industry and reform

From whatever angle we look at the situation of the working class in the developing North-East, it is the textile industry which most reflects the reality.

After the sugar industry, textiles have perhaps the

greatest relative importance in the economy of the region, corresponding to almost 30% of the industrial production of the North-East. As is happening with sugar, the textile industry for some years has been facing a grave crisis, which SUDENE, in a diagnosis made in 1961, attributes to three factors: (1) out-of-date equipment; (2) excess labour; (3) lack of finance.

The textile industry gives employment to about 30,000 workers in the whole of the North-East and contributes indirectly to more than 65,000 jobs, but this social importance has not weighed as heavily in the diagnosis as the economic factors. The great aim of the reform suggested by SUDENE is to give to the textile industry of the North-East the capacity to compete with other production centres in the country, so that it can continue with economic activity.

In brief, the reform has two objectives: modernisation of equipment and formation of skilled labour. Of the 61 factories in the North-East, more than half have already begun the reform. A wave of unemployment is created in proportion to the extent of modernisation, because technological modernising consists essentially in the replacement of mechanical machines by automatic ones, which can achieve the same production with only a quarter of the labour force. One cannot oppose the reform of the textile industry, but this does not mean that one can accept the attitude of SUDENE, which limits itself to economic factors and dismisses the social repercussions of reform.

Apart from offering no solution to the problem of unemployment caused by the textile modernisation, SUDENE is not even concerned about the matter, and feels no obligation as regards the persecutions directed by employers against workers under the pretext of reform; and this attitude persists even when injustices are committed in the name of SUDENE, by a criminal transfer of responsibility since SUDENE is outside all but technical questions. In the name of progress and development, some thousands of workers are to be thrown into misery, and no parallel decision is being taken with a view to finding new jobs for the men sacrificed.

In the Paulist textile company of Pernambuco (more than 2,000 workers in two factories) 300 permanent workers were dismissed between 9 January and 2 February, and among them five trade union leaders, a dual violation of the law of stability. The fact that all the men dismissed were workers with more than ten years of service, indicates the objective: to eliminate from the ranks the stable employees. And after the dismissals, nine clerks were employed for a few departments.

The instability of the region of Paulista, the population of which depends, for the most part, on two textile factories, condemns thousands of people to despair. The workers' trade union has tackled the situation, and with the support of the whole working class, is helping the workers who have not accepted dismissal because they are not interested in three or four million cruzeiros, but rather in a secure job and a pension in old age. These workers have taken their case to the Labour Court, where they hope to see their right to work, which is being denied to them, recognised and upheld.

At Paulista there was a trade union to defend the rights of the workers, but what of the other cases similar to this throughout the North-East, where the workers are at the mercy of their own undefended weakness? For example, 700 workers were dismissed at one time by a factory in Recife. What can they do if they have no permanent status, and have therefore no case before the Labour Court for their reinstatement?

The fact that no-one is concerned with these problems, the indifference which surrounds these human dramas, is a sign of the materialist coldness which ignores man and becomes insensitive even to hunger. It is a blindness and irresponsibility which makes it impossible to evaluate the consequences of unemployment on the life of the workers and of their families.

St James, in his letter, teaches us a lesson worth meditating: 'If a brother or sister is ill-clad and in lack of daily food, and one of you says to them, "Go in peace, be warmed and filled," without giving them the things needed for the body, what does it profit?'

VI. The Labour Court

It is in the Labour Court that we see reflected the whole situation of injustice and the lack of respect for the workers. The cases build up in their thousands, dragging on endlessly, with irretrievable loss to the workers who make their claims. There are conciliation boards with such a case-load that new applicants will have to wait for months before getting a hearing, despite the goodwill of some judges.

The workers win the majority of cases, but the time which passes in the process causes great loss and often leaves them without work and without pay. Perhaps for this reason, the employers are not worried if the workers have recourse to the court because the length of the proceedings is recompense for the possible damages they may incur. The situation is aggravated by the omission and almost total exclusion of the trade-unions, whose legal side is not very strong.

To illustrate the slow functioning of the Labour Court, the case can be quoted of the two workers (a man and a woman) in the textile industry, who worked in a Recife factory with five mechanical machines already out of date (SUDENE has set at four the reasonable number of machines per worker). The man was a model worker, who had won first place for efficiency many times in the twenty-two years since he started in the textile industry. Also the woman, with eighteen years of service, had many prizes to her credit.

In 1965, the two workers refused to accept the sixth machine which was put under their responsibility. Apart from the physical effort required by operating another machine and the breach of contract involved, they knew that production figures would go down and they would suffer financial loss. But since the firm's decisions were irreversible on principle, however just or unjust, the two workers were transferred to another factory a great distance from where they lived. They were first placed in isolation, in a department known as 'the museum'. After several weeks of threats and blackmail in order to force them to give in, they were finally allowed to work, but with more difficult machines and less pay.

In September 1965, they made an appeal to the Labour Court to be reinstated in their original factory with five machines. Meanwhile, still in 1965, they were removed from their work while the case was going on. The woman, with inadequate legal assistance, was only partially successful with her case (reinstatement, but with six machines) which did not end until February 1967, that is almost two years from the beginning of the trouble. The man is still awaiting the final judgment of the court while his family has increased in the meantime.

In this case it is not only the length of time which the court has taken to reach a decision which must be deplored, but also the injustice to the woman, which is due mainly to the exclusion of the trade union's legal department.

It is this reason also which makes it easier for the employer's legal representatives to delay the proceedings. But the lack of trade union help cannot exempt the Labour Court from all responsibility, because it is the court's duty to uphold and defend the rights of the weak and of those who have no protection. This is the first condition of justice.

The fact that the workers, despite everything, almost always win their cases proves the contempt for justice on the part of the employers, but the remedies applied by the court to rectify the situation are often rendered useless by the length of time taken to reach a decision.

The experience confirms that judges and conciliation boards are not sufficient, and the back-log of cases and processes only makes their work more difficult. Perhaps it is for this reason that the boards always try to settle disputes by amicable arrangements which invariably tend to weigh heavily against the workers.

Clearly it is essential to make the Labour Court more flexible and to increase its efficiency and improve the mechanism of just decision. The workers still have confidence in it, they depend on it to uphold their rights and guarantee their survival, they count on it to defend them against the overbearing structures in which they live. To the extent that it functions badly or too slowly, the Labour Court becomes an ally of injustice, of persecution, of the exploiting of man, and it destroys its own purpose.

The working class has confidence in the Labour Court judges, because it believes in the greatness of its mission, which is to establish in the world a little of the justice of God.

VII. The consequences

The consequences of social injustice are reflected negatively on the worker, on his family, on the community, on the trade unions and on the region itself. If the worker is the victim, the repercussions spread to all aspects of his life, destroying the foundations of the social, political and religious structure in which he lives.

Persecuted, humiliated, with no prospect of an end to his suffering, feeling himself less a human creature and more an object, the worker tends to a discouragement which produces frustration, looks to drink as an escape, and often enough accepts irresponsibility as the norm of behaviour. He remains indifferent even to the most important things in his life, such as his family, the organisation of his class, his living condition. This is to accept a personal depreciation, a conviction that the poor man has no value. It destroys the value of human feeling and the capacity to be ambitious and to believe.

The lack of hope and of faith breeds an unconscious hatred for work and for the condition of the worker. This reveals itself in a desire to lift himself out of the working class, or at least not to inflict it on his children. 'The greatest regret of my life', said a worker recently to his friends, 'is to have shown my son the machines with which I work.'

Even the young workers take on this attitude, not concerning themselves with a trade or a qualification because they do not believe in the future of the worker. The more intelligent and able of them use every opportunity, even try to emigrate to escape their situation as members of the working class, which has little value in their eyes and little hope in the future.

This crisis of values is reflected clearly in the quality of trade union leaders, since the most mature workers, who would make the best leaders, are the first victims of persecution. Fear weakens their sense of duty to their class and opens the way to compromise with the conviction that it is safer to stay on the side of the employer. All over the North-East the functioning of the trade unions, looked at from a realistic and objective viewpoint, reveals that with few exceptions the lack or alienation of strong leaders opens the door to opportunists, who are in the movement for what they can get out of it. This is a prostitution of trade unionism.

The worker and his family, who live in misery, become materialist in their conception of life, because the lack of money in their home exalts it to the highest place in their scale of values. And so we have the phenomenon of the workers most capable of engaging in the class struggle seeking their own individual promotion, even at the price of sacrificing their companions. Individual problems and difficulties press so heavily on the minds of the workers that they become incapable of discovering and reflecting upon collective problems, upon difficulties of class and community.

Closed in his own suffering, accepting it or struggling against it, the worker tends to reject every invitation to see his life in a wider perspective of community and human solidarity, because he lacks motivation and faith. This is individualism in poverty, the self-centredness which destroys the capacity to discover one's brother and to love him. Class loses meaning and community becomes a utopia, because the dynamic cell—man—is destroyed or on the way to destruction. And the primary cause is injustice.

The disintegration of the North-East, as an homogeneous region identified in the fight against underdevelopment, will increase in the measure in which development policies continue to ignore man. The potential values of the working class and of the basic communities of the region can be revealed fully and integrated into the common effort only when the workers believe in development, when it reaches them and stops coming to terms with injustice. This contempt for man creates the danger of destroying the faith of the worker of the North-East, not only in development but even in the essential human and christian values.

VIII. The reaction

Throughout this document, it is implied that every situation of social injustice in the North-East is characterised, on the one hand by the employers' attitude of almost complete contempt for their workers and on the other by the weakness of the working class which undermines their reaction to injustice and places the fittest and strongest of them in the dilemma of un-employment and starvation. For this reason the attitude of the workers is almost invariably dictated by fear of the consequences.

The more responsible leaders and workers do not accept injustice, corruption, pressure and deceit without protest. But in the main, the only choice left to the workers is to resign themselves to suffering. When the workers are capable of dignity and magnanimity therefore, and it happens more often than some people think, their attitude goes beyond the significance of isolated events and projects itself on the working class as a symbol of authenticity and fraternity. Take the attitude of the Pernambucan worker, well-known for his professional ability and dynamic activity in the trade union struggle, always in the front line of the defence of justice and interests of the working class. This worker refused the offer of a job which would have guaranteed him a salary four times greater than he was getting in his present position, so that he should not be removed from his function of effectively leading his fellow-workers.

Unfortunately and generally, the employers seem unaware of the rights and dignity of the worker, reserving for him a humiliating attitude which makes it impossible to achieve a climate of harmony and collaboration. Management decisions, even those which have the most tragic consequences for the family of the worker, are usually taken with the employer's interests in mind, and they are dictated invariably by the mistaken conviction that the worker is an adversary who must be rendered impotent or eliminated.

It would be unjust however to gloss over the exist-

162

ence of good employers, sensitive to the social drama and even disposed to work for reform. But these examples are so few that they exercise no influence whatever on the general situation of the worker.

The public authorities, in general, limit themselves to an attitude of abstention—and a reading of this document gives ample proof of this. It is no exaggeration to say that the majority of public institutions, responsible for the observance of the law and for justice in labour relations, are ineffective because of functional incapacity, lack of interest or irresponsibility. As for the politicians, their promises of dialogue and understanding, which are systematically made, are systematically forgotten.

In the midst of oppressive conditions for the working class, the trade unions, often in the hands of insincere leaders, are rarely disposed to assume their responsibility in concrete cases. Sometimes even the trade union representatives—in this case bad representatives —allow themselves to be used as agents of the employer and persuade the workers to accept solutions and agreements which serve his interests. There was a case recently of a trade union which was prepared to accept the dismissal of almost a thousand workers in a factory in Pernambuco without listening to the workers themselves.

Abandoned, without authentic leadership, begging for justice which should be theirs by right, the working class finds difficulty in trusting even the church, because, in the majority of cases, the image which they have been given links the church with the upper class, which goes to mass on Sundays, cheats them of their wages, dismisses without just cause and destroys the better elements of their society. Or they have the image which unfortunately is still presented by many priests in working-class parishes, who preach evangelical charity in their sermons and, immediately afterwards, assume attitudes of indifference towards the workers, preferring to identify themselves with the minority and privilege rather than with the majority and justice.

Only now do the workers begin to feel that something new is entering the christianity of today. And they rejoice—as we christian militants do—at seeing that the church in the North-East, through the voice of some bishops and priests, begins to take courage in the fight against injustice. In July 1966, when the bishops of the regional secretariat of the North-East (Pernambuco, Alagoas, Paraiba and Rio Grande) met at Recife, they decided to give public support to the rural and working-class movements of catholic action, signing a declaration of solidarity with the manifestoes, already published by both bodies, on the situation of suffering in their respective classes.

It is a joy to know that the church, given new life and relevance by the second Vatican Council, at last sets out on the road of identification with the causes of the people. And the ACO feels part of this church when it assumes the task—as it does now--of warning and appealing in the service of justice between men, side by side with the brethren who form with us the suffering and persecuted working class.

This rise of hope in the church must be accompanied and reinforced by discovering other positive values in the community of the North-East. The manifesto of the ACO, published on 10 March 1966, was a step in this direction. In discussing the situation of the workers in the North-East, it affirms the existence of 'positive values, of men who are concerned in every stratum of society in the North-East. There are those who respect the workers and who care about the demands of justice, who make their contribution to the fight for human advancement; who are aware of their mission to promote the common good; who sow the seed of truth by their word and example.'

These are oases of goodwill in a desert of abstention, error and social crime. But these values are the basis and starting-point for the realisation of the just society which we desire.

SUDENE, whose services to the North-East must be stressed, recognises in various publications—one of which has already been quoted—the fact that regional development tends to marginalise the mass of the workers, and for this reason it underlines the necessity of creating new dynamic instruments for the growth of the North-East, the most important of which is the policy of development centres. The main purpose of these centres is the involvement of the local communities as geographico-economic goals in the general development effort. The centres act as poles of development, with the aim of accelerating and harmonising social advancement and achieving a more equitable distribution of wealth.

This concern with the social dimension of development leads to the conclusion that there is a recognition within SUDENE of the serious alienation of the people, and this confirms the fact that there are responsible men who are prepared to assist in perfecting or changing the techniques hitherto used and the philosophy which has so far predominated, both tending danger-ously to capitalist materialism.

In the political field—both legislative and executive —there are also to be found men who feel the re-sponsibility of their office, even if at times they lack the courage to put into practice what they preach with conviction. In art, in literature, among all who create and manipulate public opinion, there are some who stoke a permanent fire of protest, of clarification and of watchfulness. The number of christians who discover and accept concrete responsibilities in their lives and in their surroundings is increasing every day, and they respond by a conscious effort to christianise and humanise the structures and relationships which govern the lives of men.

The hope of a better world must be based on these values, which are the only effective weapons in the battle for a just solution. To them are directed the cry of anguish and of justice which issues from this docu-ment.

But our greatest hopes are still turned to the working class itself, whose capacity for suffering indicates a reserve of moral and spiritual force which must be discovered and evaluated by the workers themselves, so that unity may give them strength and awareness, so that brotherhood may overcome their instinct of self-defence which narrows reaction and ambition to the dimensions of the individual, so that human solidarity may give life to the great community of those who have only arms, intelligence and heart to fulfil themselves as men and as sharers in the work of creation.

It is essential that the examples of human and chris-tian greatness, given by the more authentic leaders, should bear fruit in the womb of the working class, so that a collective and unifying consciousness may strengthen the unity of the workers. The response of the worker in a factory at Pernambuco, who was forbidden to collect the subscriptions of his trade union colleagues within the factory itself, must not remain an isolated cry: 'If I must choose between dying as a man and dying as a coward, I shall die as a man.'

Support must be given to resolute and courageous trade union leaders—the case of the Paulista trade unionist comes to mind—and their number multiplied in every professional category, because only in this way will the trade union establish itself as an instrument of unity and a weapon in the fight for collective advancement. Attitudes of firmness and confidence must permeate every nucleus of the community if solutions are to be found and their application to be directed by the workers themselves.

Finally and above all, it is imperative that the solidarity of the working class should be expressed in individual attitudes between worker and worker—like the unemployed bricklayer in Paraiba, who was offered two days' work and gave one to a companion in similar circumstances—and in collective attitudes, when the interests and needs of the majority must orientate the behaviour of all.

Fraternal solidarity is the thread which links the whole history of the working class in every continent and in every country. Witness to solidarity abounds in the North-East and shows that the working class is alive and capable of forming a great movement of unity based not only on the contribution of its members but above all on the demands of right and of justice.

IX. The North-East and the Third World

Underdevelopment constitutes a chain of solidarity in the modern world, where two-thirds of humanity lives in sub-human conditions, especially in Asia, Africa and Latin America. So much has underdevelopment become an international concern that the church has appropriated the expression of Cardinal Feltin, archbishop of Paris: 'Development is the new name for peace.'

Among this two-thirds, humanity suffers starvation, struggles in unemployment, lives in destitute houses, lacks the means of defence and improvement, lives in subjection to a privileged minority, has no easy access to education, does not share in the wealth of production, in short, lives in that unmerited misery already denounced to the world in 1891 by Pope Leo XIII in the encyclical *Rerum Novarum.*

In Latin America, which forms a great part of the underdeveloped area of the world—the Third World, as it is popularly called—half the population must be satisfied with a fifth of the total production, while 5% of the population gets 20% of the same production. Another aspect of this distribution of wealth consists in the fact that half the arable land of Latin America belongs to only 1·5% of farming proprietors.

In Brazil at least 70% of the population over five years of age is illiterate and this percentage is even greater in some areas of the North-East. In Venezuela 50% of the national income is enjoyed by 12% of the families. In Brazil 63% of the national income benefits 17% of the population. In 1960, the average spending capacity of a Latin-American citizen was 350 dollars per year, that of a West European 1,013 and a North American 2,785 dollars.

It must be added moreover that the rich countries spend large sums on armaments. According to research done by Russian and American experts, the expenditure on arms and defence in 1961 reached 120 billion dollars, enough to educate 250 million children.

There is food, money and technical abundance in a small part of the world, while the great majority suffer hunger, misery, illiteracy and lack of professional skill.

In the last ten years the countries of the Third World have become aware of their situation in relation to the rest of the world and have begun the struggle against underdevelopment. The word 'development' has spread like a message of redemption and it has acquired its greatest significance in Latin America.

The Brazilian North-East has become a problem region in the orbit of Latin America and a centre of special attention. With the creation of SUDENE in 1959, an experiment in economic development was begun, which is today regarded as an example for the whole continent of Latin America and even for the whole Third World.

Experts from various countries of the world come to the North-East to see the work that is being done in the economico-social field. Those who direct the development process in this region bear the responsibility of avoiding errors and distortions, which could easily be reproduced in other areas and countries where policies and programmes are based on our experience. Frequent and honest evaluation of the work which is being done to identify and correct imbalance is essential if we are to perfect the model of development in the North-East.

Since development and injustice are incompatible, at least ethically, it is most urgent that the North-East should become fully aware of the social disorder which persists and spreads in the region, because a development which does not serve the collective good is useless.

The demands of justice in our day must acquire total dimensions, because development means striving for justice and peace, struggling to eliminate the structural defects and ideas caused by the unjust and inequitable distribution of the goods essential for the fulfilment of every man and of every people.

Pope Paul VI, in a letter sent to the Latin-American Episcopal Council meeting at Mar del Plata, said: 'Development must be integral if it is to be authentic, raising up the whole person and the whole of humanity ... guided by a principle of unity.' The bishops, for their part, stated at the close of the meeting that 'the integration of the whole of Latin America is irreversibly in process. It constitutes an indispensable instrument for the harmonious development of the region and marks a fundamental stage in the movement for the unification of the human family'.

The solidarity of the Third World in the fight for justice within the great international society is thus countersigned by the desire for unity. The underdeveloped races and peoples—white, black, yellow, Latin-American, African and Asiatic—are united not only by the same problems but, above all, by a self-awakening in the struggle for justice, development and peace. And the church, through the second Vatican Council and through the voice of the pope and of many bishops, is leading this awareness of human solidarity, which will distinguish the twentieth century.

The North-East must acquire that greatness which will enable it to understand development not as a mere exercise in theory and technique, but as a common endeavour to construct a more just and more human society, as God wills it.

X. Self-awakening

The basis of our appeal is the dignity of man, the image of God, as a person and as a community ('let us make man to our image and likeness', Gen. 1 : 27). But the greatest ideas are of no value whatever unless they become part of life, part of our attitudes, our choices, part of our daily routine. Otherwise we give a mere notional assent and exclude the dynamic force of ideas which may concern the dignity of another man or another group.

Reality today invites us to examine our consciences, beginning with an evaluation of our words of commitment and obligation. Development is the commonest and most fashionable word today in the North-East. It is a word full of meaning and hope, because it translates 'peace'. It is a perfect response to the mission entrusted to men by God: 'Subdue the earth' (Gen 1 : 28).

Thanks to development, and to the faith, intelligence and imagination of many who understand it, it has been possible to elaborate and execute plans which have opened up prospects of future well-being to the North-East. But the facts narrated in this document, the enormous suffering of the people, the lack of participation in the development, seem to indicate that technology, and perhaps even the financial interests of the plans, have forgotten man. The gospel reminds us that 'the sabbath was made for man, not man for the sabbath' (Mk 2:27).

The basic question is this: what is the hierarchy of values which has determined and still determines the elaboration and execution of development plans? Is it man today, or a vague idea of humanity tomorrow? Is it the community—every community—or the strengthening of powerful economic groups?

Is it to promote man and improve his work, or is it the appreciation of capital? Social advancement and peace, or a statistical rise in production? 'If man is not given priority, development is impossible', said the North-East bishops in a joint declaration on 14 July 1966. These bishops are applying to the North-East the principles laid down in the *Pastoral Constitution on the Church in the Modern World*, where it is affirmed that 'believers and non-believers are almost unanimous in holding that man is the centre and culminating point of all the things on earth'. The question arises therefore: is man the supreme point of reference in the development of the North-East?

Is it man as he is today, with all that he knows and all that he is capable of? With the time he needs to prepare himself intelligently and freely for the new techniques? With his basic right to work? Man with his right, which is a fundamental necessity, to a life worthy of himself and of his family? With the right and the possibility of participating in plans and decisions? Man with his freedom to choose his state of life? With his

172

indispensable place in society? With his right to culture and to the culture proper to his environment?

On the other hand, according to the christian order, man cannot be separated from the community, from the society in which he lives and participates. 'It is clear', says the council document quoted, 'that on account of the social character of man, the fulfilment of the human person and the development of society are interdependent.' And it adds: 'since social life cannot be added sporadically to man, he evolves in all his qualities through communication with others, by means of mutual obligations and dialogue with his brothers'. Therefore what is affirmed of the person of man must apply to every community, which must be responsible for dialogue and free to engage in it.

The problem again arises: does development in the North-East take the community into consideration? The present communities and those which must arise in the future? The communities with their recognised natural leaders? The communities with their own existing structures? Their own cultural heritage? Their right to decide their own future? The communities with the right and duty to assume the task of their own development through a conscious participation?

Honesty compels us to state that the working class is always the most humiliated and that trade unionism is obstructed; that the organisations of the workers have been alienated and up to now excluded from the process of development, even from questions which concern them directly. Surely this is emptying, denying and destroying the sense of community and its value?

These negations of man and of the community are a negation of God. The lack of justice, of truth and of love disfigures and damages the image of God. To injure man and the community is to injure God. If what we desire is the construction of an authentically christian society and civilisation, we are bound by our faith to help every group to become a community, that is a living centre of human and creative relationships. And therefore we insist on the necessity to reflect on the values of man and of society in the light of the gospel and of the teaching of Christ.

Christ's behaviour reveals a deep respect for the human person. We see him with children, with the sick, with the apostles ... what counts for Christ are not the structures or the laws, but the sick man with all he needs for his body, the child with his wonder and affection, the apostle eager to understand and to act.

The morality of the gospels is summed up in the command of fraternal love, perfectly illustrated in Christ's attitude towards the sabbath.

His rebukes to the pharisees have no other meaning than to affirm that man is the supreme value. But Christ never separated man from the community. He himself chose a people, a nation, a family, to realise himself as the saviour of mankind. In his actions and attitudes, immortalised in the gospels, we see the great importance which he always gave to the city (Nazareth, Capernaum, Jerusalem ...), to the market-place, to the group of fishermen, to the community of the apostles. The gospels therefore teach us that the church cannot be established where there is no community. The church is born of the community of Jews, of the community of fishermen, of slaves, etc. 'From the beginning of salvation history, he has chosen men not just as individuals but as members of a certain community. Revealing his mind to them, God called these chosen ones "his people" (Ex 3 : 7–12), and, furthermore, made a covenant with them on Sinai' (*The Church in the Modern World,* 32).

This is why the ACO, with its mission to participate in the evangelisation of the modern world, claims that this world must be a free and responsible community. There can be no other goal of development.

XI. Time for action

Some may wonder how, in the name of the gospel, we speak of sin in hard and almost revolutionary language. In this however we have in mind the appeal made by Paul VI in his address to the diplomatic corps on 17 January 1967:

> The church cannot remove herself from temporal affairs, because the temporal is the activity of men, and all that concerns men concerns the church. A disembodied church, separated from the world, would no longer be the church of Jesus Christ, the church of the incarnate Word. The church, on the contrary, interests herself closely in every generous endeavour which helps to set humanity on the road to heaven, but also in the search for well-being, for justice, for peace, for happiness on earth.

Our first duty as active christians in the working-class environment, is to speak the truth without fear and without exaggeration. The second, common to all men of goodwill, is to face the whole truth and to accept the demands which it makes.

If there is hunger (and there is), food must be demanded; if there is massive unemployment (and there is), demands must be made for new jobs to be created; if there is cheating over wages, persecution of people, crushing of human dignity, elimination of leaders, destruction of the community, humiliation of man (and all this exists in the developing North-East) we must cry out for justice and for respect. The problems raised here demand definite attitudes, action on the part of the community and of each member.

Example must first be given by the authorities, who are entrusted with the responsibility of promoting the common good by every legitimate means. This implies a greater duty of response on the part of those who need help if they are to fulfil themselves as human persons. The common good can only mean the good of all: and this imposes on our rulers the urgent duty of correcting, by appropriate action, the injustice of the present situation in which few succeed in satisfying rights proper to all. We cannot understand, for example, how it is possible to tolerate unemployment and the closing of factories without a rigorous examination of the real causes; nor the attitude of indifference of the public authorities towards the drama and misery of the workers who are sacked in great numbers from their jobs. The common good imposes a social responsibility on capital and therefore on the government, especially in a region like the North-East, where the official stimulus is so often given to capital itself.

It is binding on governments to issue laws which correspond to the real aspirations of the people, and above all to use all the power invested in them to ensure the application of these laws, especially when they aim at reforming out-dated, unjust and inhuman structures. In the specific case of the North-East, the facts impose on the constituted authority a courageous policy of creating more jobs, of giving incentives to food production, a policy which inevitably implies agrarian reform.

SUDENE has particular responsibilities, being a body which enjoys the confidence of the region for the seriousness of its work. If an investment policy geared to the infrastructure was justified in the first years, now is the time to modify the relative priority of the various sectors of its programme, so that a philosophy which will humanise development may prevail. It is time for SUDENE to assume command of the structural reforms of the region, counting on its natural position of technical leadership which is respected not only in the North-East but in the whole country. It is time for an integrated development strategy which will ensure balance in economic growth—the imbalance between agriculture and industrialisation is particularly in mind—and for the creation of mechanisms for the equitable distribution of income, so that progress and prosperity will not come only to the few. And it is time moreover to integrate into development the institution's department of human resources. There are some sectors in this department which concern the working class, such as education, training, community activity.

Experts and technicians at all levels, and especially those who direct development programmes, must be reminded that they are the hope for a solution to the problems of today. They are entrusted with the task of placing technology at the service of man and of putting pressure on the institutions in which they work, so that these may respect and face up to the social demands of development. However mathematical the theories may be, the final end of all plans is man, and experts must incorporate in their professional formation the concern to discover man in and through technology.

The anguish and insecurity of the workers demand that a vehement appeal be made to the employers to try to discover the worker's contribution to the wealth of their undertaking. This may be the easiest road to the discovery of the human value of the worker and to his treatment with respect and justice as a collaborator in a common goal.

A new and renewing force in the collective body of the employers is possible if those among them, who are concerned with social justice and who contribute in a practical way to a society which respects the dignity and rights of man, unite and work for this end.

But within each undertaking there is an undeniable responsibility which falls on the immediate superiors of the workers. They must see in the worker not only an element of production under their control, but above all a man, the head of a family, with need of support, of understanding and of respect. These industrial heads must assume the mission of creating and defending justice and consider it their duty not to look only to the interests of the management, but also to the interests of the workers. Only in this way will the factory acquire dimensions of community and help the worker to assume all the responsibilities of his life.

If the trade unions are to take up their proper task in the development of the North-East on behalf of the working class, they must first be transformed into an authentic means of promotion and struggle for the worker, opening themselves to all his problems and giving to their function as vindicators a human dimension. Up to now, apart from other more serious omissions, the majority of the trade unions in the North-East is contented with and limited to a discussion of the wages question, when so many other grave problems are crying out for the attention of the workers' organisation.

It is up to the trade unions to break the marginalisation of the working class in the process of development. They have an initial obligation to be informed about the matter, precisely so that they may inform, instruct and arouse the people whom they represent. All this is part of the effort which the trade unions must make in the organisation of the community of the North-East if they are to assume the position of importance which is theirs by right and by the natural demands of equilibrium. The exercise of pressure, whenever the circumstances demand it, is implied in the legitimate function of the trade union, a pressure which is the counterpart of that exercised by capital and the capitalist class on governments and on the life of the country.

For every worker we have a message of faith. It is essential to believe, to believe in ourselves, in our dignity, in our capacity, in our value. For each one of us there is the work of professional and human upgrading. And this must flow out into participation in the life of the working class. We must overcome the limitations of individualism, so that each of us may acquire a vision of community, without which it will be impossible to strengthen the trade union and defend it from exploiters, opportunists and intriguers. In other words, it is imperative that every worker should assume his responsibility towards the family, work, class and neighbourhood. Every responsible worker must be committed.

It is with great trust, in this document bristling with demands, that we manifest our faith in the church, and we address a vigorous appeal to the bishops, to priests and to the laity. There is a challenge which the whole church must accept: to renew friendship with the working class. It is a challenge from within, an intimate challenge whose greatness lies in the church's capacity to know and understand the working class, their values and their problems. A church truly integrated in the world and identified with men—as the council has desired—will not merit the charge of being the opium of the people, because it will be transformed into a hope and a source of life, the continuing presence of Christ who created it for this purpose. The working class will accept and believe and participate in the church, the mother and teacher of all and not only of some. The working class looks to the church for its rightful place in her womb, above all in her pastoral care and in her concern.

We look to the church to animate, with the purity and energy of the gospel, all the forces of the North-East which strive for the ordered development of man. Among them we include the catholic action movements, who have as their primary duty an evangelisation embodied in the reality of life.

There is a heavy responsibility on lay christians from every stratum of society to involve the church and christianity in life and in the problems of humanity. The technician, the politician, the teacher, the student, the supervisor, the scientist, the intellectual, in other words all those who accept the truth of the gospel in their lives and who are called to play their part in the defence of man and of justice. The solutions to the problems of the people depend on these laity. Our faith —faith in God and in man—demands action. It does not dictate concrete solutions to our problems but it does teach us the christian approach to life and to involvement in it.

Finally, a message of hope for the working class, our class, which has been the inspiration of this document. This is intended to be more than a message; it is a call to hope, for without hope we cannot believe in the cause of the workers nor in the value of their social class. But hope is coming, and it will be strengthened in so far as every worker, from the most highly skilled to the humblest and most defenceless, participates fully in the cause and in the life of the working class.

There is a message of transforming struggle in christianity; the death and resurrection of Christ were aimed at the transformation of the world. This gives us the certainty that God is not only with the suffering but also with those who fight for the dignity and fulfilment of the most perfect work of creation: man. This is a further reason for rallying all the forces, all the responsible individuals and groups of the North-East to combine their efforts in an endeavour to achieve the development and advancement of every man in the North-East and of the whole community.

Only with the union of all its active and effective nuclei will the North-East fulfil its mission to be a region in course of development in Brazil and in the Third World.

DATE DUE

~~JUN 2 78~~			
~~JUN 2 8~~			
GAYLORD			PRINTED IN U.S.A.